Backs
Against
the Wall

Urban-Oriented Colleges and Universities and the Urban Poor and Disadvantaged

by Pastora San Juan Cafferty and Gail Spangenberg

|| FORD FOUNDATION
|| Series on Higher Education in the Cities

One of a series of reports on activities supported by the Ford Foundation. A complete list of Foundation publications may be obtained from the Ford Foundation's Office of Reports, 320 East 43 Street, New York, N.Y. 10017.

Library of Congress Cataloging in Publication Data

Cafferty, Pastora San Juan.
  Backs against the wall.

  (Series on higher education in the cities; 3)
  Includes bibliographical references.
  1. Socially handicapped children—Education (Higher)—United States. 2. Educational equalization—United States. I. Spangenberg, Gail. II. Title. III. Series.
  LC4069.6.C33 1983   371.96'7   82-25124
  ISBN 0-916584-22-4

Contents

Foreword

In the coming years there will be no more important challenge to institutions of higher education than to preserve and extend their commitment to the poor and disadvantaged. That is particularly true of the cities, where so many people in need of help are concentrated—racial and ethnic minorities, unemployed youth, recent immigrants, and others. Their education—in the schools and beyond—is critical to their futures and to that of the cities as well. In considerable part, the solution to many of the problems of cities depends on educating the people who live and work in them.

In higher education, this job falls primarily to urban-oriented colleges and universities—institutions in the central cities whose educational mission, whether by charter or default, is to serve the cities' people. Their undergraduate enrollments reflect that orientation, and because these institutions are based in the city and serve such a diverse range of people and needs, they have special problems that need to be much more widely recognized and addressed. An alarming gap remains between those served and those locked out of higher education in the cities. The future well-being of the cities, their colleges and universities, and their people depend in large part on narrowing the gap (and remaining firm in the resolve to do so) despite financial constraints and other obstacles.

In 1978, and again in mid-1980, the Ford Foundation's concern about these issues prompted it to make a series of grants totaling some $1.1 million to help urban-oriented colleges and universities—and those who make and shape policy affecting them—to examine and work on undergraduate services and programs for the inner-city poor and disadvantaged. The focus of the overall program was on problems most directly affecting educational access and success for these people. From the standpoint of what current and potential students need, the main problems seemed to be: (1) remediation of basic

5

skills, including training in English as a second language; (2) academic counseling, guidance, and diagnosis of learning problems; and (3) information services that help students learn about the array of education institutions and programs available in their cities, to choose wisely among them, and then to wend their way through the maze of procedures, requirements, and forms involved in getting admitted to college and obtaining financial aid.

In order to help colleges and universities provide a fuller range of such services and programs, the Foundation designed its grants to emphasize inter-institutional planning and the sharing of resources. Given the economic facts of life today, institutions of higher education are challenged to do more educationally with fewer resources. It is no secret that most institutions have a natural inclination to resolve their difficulties in their own separate ways. But in order to deal effectively with the problems of higher education in the cities, there needs to be a much greater willingness—by colleges, universities, schools, communities, and city government agencies—to join together around common problems, develop solutions cooperatively, and share resources.

Six of the eight grants the Foundation made in 1978 were the result of a search in which some fifty-five urban-oriented colleges and universities in thirteen major cities participated.* A seventh grant established a national communications network of urban-oriented colleges and universities. Under an eighth grant, one of a series examining how government policy affects the participation of low-income and other needy people in higher education, the Washington Office of the College Board conducted a study of the obstacles to the full use of federal student aid and loan programs by the urban poor.

To share the results of these grants the Foundation is publishing a series of booklets collectively called *Higher Education in the Cities.* The College Board study appeared in February 1981 under the title *Student Aid and the Urban Poor.* A second report, entitled *A Tale of Three Cities: Boston, Birmingham, Hartford* (1981), described efforts to improve educational services for the poor and disadvantaged in the three cities. The efforts included outreach to high schools, minority community groups, and adult learners; tutoring in basic skills; programs in English as a second language; and the use of retired teachers to coach elementary and junior high school students in reading, mathematics, and English.

---

* Five of the six projects received supplemental support; the sixth operated under the original grant. For a listing of these grants, and related grants made subsequently, see Appendix B.

6

In this third report, *Backs Against the Wall: Urban-Oriented Colleges and Universities and the Urban Poor and Disadvantaged*, Pastora San Juan Cafferty of the University of Chicago and the National Opinion Research Center and Gail Spangenberg, an independent consultant and former foundation program officer, assess the results of this set of Foundation grants. Noting that there are hundreds of urban-oriented colleges and universities in U.S. cities and their immediate environs, the authors examine the problems such institutions face in trying to help the poor and disadvantaged overcome multiple deprivations and begin to gain control of their own lives. They conclude with recommendations for addressing these problems.

Clearly, the issues raised and the recommendations made in this report must be viewed in light of changing conditions and contexts. Today there is vigorous debate about the federal government's role in education—the extent, for example, to which it should support student financial aid. And, of course, enrollments in urban higher education institutions are changing from city to city, both in size and diversity. Despite these evolving circumstances, the issues raised and the recommendations offered by Dr. Cafferty and Ms. Spangenberg are still to the point and merit serious consideration. In the meantime, we hope this report will help practitioners and policy makers shape the role of higher education in city life and help brighten the future of American cities.

EDWARD J. MEADE, JR.

Ford Foundation
February 1983

Introduction

In no country is higher education so widely available to so large a share of people as it is in the United States. During the past two decades no country has worked harder than the United States to extend opportunities for higher education to the poor and disadvantaged. Despite this effort, a large gap remains between those served by higher education and those not served. And now, in the early 1980s, economic pressures and a mood of conservatism are beginning to narrow access to higher education for those disadvantaged and unconventional students who were beginning to be reached with increasing frequency and success. Nowhere is this recent downturn more apparent than in the inner cities of the nation's large urban centers—where the poor, minorities, unemployed youth, recent immigrants, and other underprivileged groups are so heavily concentrated.

The job of educating city dwellers, particularly the poor and disadvantaged, falls largely to those colleges and universities based in the city and primarily dedicated to serving the people of the city. These urban-oriented colleges and universities are an essential resource both to the city and to its people. For persons who are poor and disadvantaged, these institutions can open the door to fuller participation in the mainstream economy. The health and well-being of both cities and their people depend in large part on the improved delivery of education to people at all levels of city life.

In this report, we discuss problems faced by urban-oriented institutions generally. We also describe the experience of such institutions in six cities during a grant program sponsored by the Ford Foundation and summarize the results of research undertaken with Ford funding. (See the Foreword and Appendix B.) The views, analyses, and conclusions presented are our own. They are based on three years of extensive involvement in the grant projects and on consultations with a wide range of people—not only those who make policy but also those

9

who work in the trenches—in colleges and universities, in community and governmental agencies, in urban-planning organizations, and in the schools. Those who took part in a Foundation conference in May 1980 contributed greatly to our synthesis of the issues, and their thoughts about the problems and their solutions have helped to shape our own. (For a list of participants in the May 1980 conference see Appendix A.)

This paper is concerned primarily with two questions:

1. What, specifically, are the problems of urban-oriented colleges and universities in meeting the educational needs of the urban poor and disadvantaged?

2. What is being done, and what can be done in the future, to address those problems?

One premise underlying our discussion is that the nation, the cities, and urban-oriented institutions themselves cannot afford to let the problems go unattended, even though most of them resist simple and quick solutions. The cities cannot expect continued vitality and a stable future unless they have an educated citizenry and unless ways can be found to strengthen the performance and extend the outreach of the institutions whose job it is to provide higher education to city people.

Another underlying premise is that successive generations of Americans will continue to congregate in the cities. Cities have provided access to the economic mainstream for more than 200 years and will continue to do so in the future. As our society and economy are affected by the forces of technological change and mass living, the need for higher education in the cities will be ever greater to assure participation in the economy and in other benefits of postindustrial America. Moreover, the economics of the inner cities and the circumstances of the people who live in them require that higher education be available where the people are—that is, in the cities themselves.

Urban-Oriented Colleges and Universities: Characteristics and Problems

As a group, urban-oriented colleges and universities have a number of common features. They are located in the inner cities of the major metropolitan areas of the country and are fundamentally community- and service-oriented. Some are community colleges, other are four-year colleges and universities, and still others are complex systems providing programs at all educational levels. Whether public or private, they are largely nonresidential. Their primary purpose is to educate the local resident population, particularly at the undergraduate level, and their enrollments reflect that orientation. Generally, they are not highly prestigious or highly selective in their admissions—in fact, many are committed to a policy of open admissions. For the most part, they do not have national reputations or many students drawn from beyond the city's limits. Although some have excellent graduate and professional programs, most of their students are undergraduates of widely varying ages, attendance patterns, and educational needs. They include working adults, members of minorities, poor people, persons with low levels of educational preparedness, and, increasingly, immigrants whose native language is not English.

The heterogeneity of their student bodies and the numbers of part-time and educationally disadvantaged students they serve can cause these institutions to have complex educational processes. They are required to work much more extensively in the remediation of basic skills than are other institutions of higher education. Because of a large influx of new immigrants into some urban centers, the educational institutions there are heavily involved in teaching English as a second language, in bilingual education, or in both.

Because the phrase "urban-oriented colleges and universities" is not precise in its meaning, it is difficult if not impossible to know the exact number of institutions that fall into this category. But we know there are some 300 in U.S. cities with populations of at least 100,000 and hundreds more in the metropolitan environs of these major cities and in cities of lower population.

Wayne State University, Miami-Dade Community College, and the colleges of the City University of New York are easily identified as urban-oriented institutions of higher education. So is the University of the District of Columbia, which is one of numerous institutions created specifically to serve inner-city people. Boston University and the University of Hartford are probably less easily identified as such because of the makeup of their undergraduate enrollments. Both, however, serve large numbers of central-city poor and disadvantaged, and both provide a variety of important services and training programs for their cities. The University of Massachusetts at Boston, like many other institutions that are part of a state system, is in the process of defining its urban mission.

According to our definition, institutions that draw their students primarily from national and international population groups—for example, the University of Chicago, Columbia University, and George Washington University—are not urban-oriented, although they are physically located in the city. To be sure, they make major contributions to the welfare of the city as employers and they work to stem deterioration in their neighborhoods. For example, the University of Chicago has not only stabilized property values in the Hyde Park section of the city where it is situated, but it is also the largest single private employer in Chicago. In addition, by providing research and technical assistance to government and to community agencies, these and other city-based institutions of higher education contribute to the well-being of the city, and they often provide such essential services as hospitals and clinics and legal assistance for the poor. But unlike urban-oriented colleges and universities they do not exist primarily to educate residents of their cities. Their research, teaching, and service are generally independent of the community in which they are located. More importantly for our purposes, the majority of their students are not residents of the city and their educational programs are not shaped by the needs of the local population.

In short, many of the problems of urban-oriented colleges and universities derive from their being both *in* and *of* the city—they are tied organically to it, to its people, and to their problems.

WHAT ARE THE PROBLEMS?

To a great extent, the problems of urban-oriented colleges and universities grow out of the problems faced by the cities they are in. For example, in the last decade or so middle-income people have fled to the suburbs and waves of new immigrants and poor people have moved in. These population shifts have had dramatic consequences for the cities, resulting in heavier concentrations of the poor and disadvantaged and sharp reductions in the city tax base. As more and more service, technical, and professional jobs have opened up, those who are unskilled and uneducated have become less and less employable. And as unemployment rises, crime increases. A weak national economy, combined with halfhearted federal and state efforts to restore the cities, is taking its toll: rapid mass transit and other services begin to falter and decline; neighborhoods start to decay and empty, particularly in the large cities of the Northeast. City schools, unable to cope with the impact of population shifts and economic austerity, question old standards of performance and fail to find new ones. Students become dispirited and, depending on their temperament, withdraw, rebel, or drop out entirely.

These problems inevitably affect the fortunes and capabilities of urban-oriented colleges and universities and make it difficult for them to serve those in the city with special learning needs. Moreover, internal factors such as lack of strong and committed institutional leadership, academically conservative faculty attitudes, outmoded instructional approaches, and simple inertia contribute to the problems the institutions face. In addition, external factors such as federal and state aid and funding policies often have an unintended negative effect on the institutions and on the rate at which poor and disadvantaged people participate in higher education.

The specific problems of urban-oriented institutions of higher education cluster around ten interrelated focal points.

Underfunding. Because of their urban location, institutions most likely to serve the disadvantaged and poor generally have higher overhead costs than other institutions of higher education. The diverse needs of their learners require an array of expensive programs and services—remediation of basic skills, English as a second language, guidance and counseling. At the same time, states use full-time equivalency (FTE) formulas that often penalize urban-oriented colleges and universities. These formulas fail to account adequately for large enrollments of part-time students or to recognize that the costs of programs and services needed by such students do not decrease in direct proportion to the number of credit hours the students carry. Also, many of the special programs carry no credit and are underfunded because they do not fit credit-based funding formulas.

Cutbacks in Vital Programs and Services. The steady flow of state and federal funds in the 1960s and early 1970s led many public urban-oriented institutions to expand rapidly in order to accommodate new kinds of students. During the same period, other institutions were specifically created to serve inner-city people. Reductions in government funds in the last few years have forced the institutions to eliminate or curtail many of their essential services and programs, even as the need for them has increased. Yet the decisions to cut back have frequently been made without the planning and evaluation needed to assure an equitable allocation of resources, to preserve educational access and opportunity, and to promote the most efficient use of available resources.

As might have been predicted, open admissions and basic skills programs and related services, so crucial to disadvantaged learners, have been the first to suffer cutbacks. At the City University of New York (CUNY), to use one dramatic example, curtailment of open admissions in 1975, combined with the loss of the university's "no-tuition" policy, resulted by 1978 in the loss of some 72,000 students[1]; the great majority were the educationally and economically disadvantaged. A pioneer in open admissions, CUNY still provides programs in basic skills and other special services for New York's disadvantaged learners, and it also maintains a modified open enrollment policy. But the burden of both now falls more heavily upon the university's community colleges. CUNY is a special situation, to be sure, but this pattern of reduced access is repeated in small and large urban-oriented institutions across the country.

High Attrition. The attrition rates of educationally disadvantaged students in urban-oriented institutions are alarmingly high. According to officials of the University of the District of Columbia, for instance, only about 1,500 of the 7,000 freshmen enrolled there in 1978 are expected to graduate. Many other such institutions report similar attrition rates.

Failures in the School System. The dropout rate in urban high schools is also alarmingly high. The increasing number of dropouts, when added to the growing number of high school graduates who have serious deficiencies in basic skills, is creating an ever larger group of undereducated inner-city youth. Marginally prepared for any role in a changing society, these young people spend a good deal of time "hanging out" on the streets, giving up (sooner or later) all hopes for employment, and venting their frustrations in various antisocial activities. Their best hope for overcoming their multiple deprivations and for finding employment is further education—*if*, of course, the

14

programs they need are available and *if* they can be reached and motivated to seek them out.

Student Poverty. Despite federal, state, and institutional financial aid, urban residents at the lowest steps of the income ladder are still unable to afford a college education—for reasons that have to do in part with the complexities of the aid systems and the application forms themselves, problems that are discussed beginning on page 47.

Confused Mission. Many—though certainly not all—urban-oriented institutions of higher education have a confused sense of mission. They suffer from a kind of institutional schizophrenia, "being pulled one way by the prerogatives and respectabilities of traditional academe and the other by the urgent and unconventional needs of their communities for higher education and education services."[2] Thus, the attitude still prevails that in providing special programs for underprepared students—in basic skills, for example—the proper business of higher education is being subverted. Another common attitude is that education for undergraduate students should be designed to prepare them for graduate study at some prestigious institution rather than for employment, which is the real need of most students enrolled in urban-oriented institutions.

Ignoring the Needs of the Local Community. Caught up in their day-to-day activities and often tending to emulate traditional academe, urban-oriented institutions often fail to recognize fully the nature and extent of their ties to the city; for example, they seldom conduct systematic research on the educational and employment needs of their urban communities. Such research must be carried on regularly if the institutions' educational offerings are to fit reality.

Overprizing Traditional Ways. The faculty of most of the institutions tend to favor established ways of doing things for established groups of people. Yet poor, disadvantaged students require vastly different instructional approaches. To relate effectively to these students, changes in both curricula and faculty attitudes are urgently needed. For many reasons, ranging from job security to educational theory, such changes are fiercely resisted.

Undervaluing Institutional Cooperation. Like most institutions of higher education, urban-oriented colleges and universities generally prefer to go it alone. The tendency is to compete for scarce resources—including students—rather than to cooperate with other colleges and universities, local business and industry, community organizations, and local secondary schools. The present competitive environment is academically destructive and financially wasteful.

Failure to Communicate. As a result of these tensions and tendencies, the institutions do not do a very good job of communicating their needs and their mission to the public, to state and federal legislators, or even among themselves. This failure has negative implications for their funding and for their enrollment size and composition.

GENERAL CAVEATS

The great majority of people with whom we have talked about urban-oriented institutions of higher education over the past few years agree on the problems and special characteristics of their institutions as sketched above. Moreover, both the problems and the characteristics have been confirmed in data collected from some 280 urban-oriented colleges and universities by the American Association of State Colleges and Universities in a national project funded by the Ford Foundation.*

It should be noted, however, that not everyone is sympathetic to the idea of focusing attention on urban-oriented institutions. Some argue that the discussion should focus on higher education of the urban poor or of any central-city residents in general. They rightly point out that all institutions of higher education are in trouble today and that most are called upon, to some degree, to serve the poor and disadvantaged.

The argument has merit but, as this paper shows, urban-oriented colleges and universities differ significantly in mission and circumstance from their urban and suburban neighbors. If the nation's efforts to revitalize its cities are to produce lasting results, these must include a far greater understanding and awareness of the role and importance of these urban-oriented institutions in the life of the cities.

Another argument we have heard is that urban-oriented colleges and universities, like all institutions of higher education, have several functions. In addition to teaching, some also conduct major research and provide a variety of noneducational services for the community and municipal governments. This argument usually concludes by saying that it is just as important to be concerned about the development

---

* The results of the project are reported in a series of publications entitled *Connections*, published by the American Association of State Colleges and Universities, One Dupont Circle, Suite 700, Washington, D.C. 20036.

of these functions as it is to worry about the institution's basic educational functions.

This point of view is also right. Urban-oriented institutions of higher education do make a major contribution to the city's affairs and to the quality of its life when they study such problems as crime in the streets or delivery of social services. They contribute similarly when they provide technical assistance to municipal governments and community organizations or legal and medical services to the needy. But improving these activities will not directly improve the educational prospects of the inner-city poor and disadvantaged. Their immediate need for access is to undergraduate education, with all that implies by way of special programs and services. Their needs make the educational function of the institutions a top priority. Indeed, it could be argued that the quality of the institutions' research and service is dependent upon the strength of their basic educational performance, particularly at the undergraduate level.

We are not the first to stress the importance of urban-oriented colleges and universities and their unique educational service to the cities. Others have been trying to make the same point for years. Nor are we the first to underscore the central importance of undergraduate education for all people of a city. In an article in *Compact* magazine, Thomas Robinson, vice president for academic affairs at Pace University in New York City, noted that no urban-oriented institution of higher education should "forget for a moment its fundamental reason for being: the transmission of knowledge."[3] He went on to say that the future health of these institutions depends more than anything else on maintaining strength in undergraduate education and turning the undergraduate enterprise increasingly to the needs of "young people from lower socioeconomic families, white, black, and Hispanic."[4]

Finally, some thoughts are in order on the subject of open admissions. One of the participants in the Foundation's May 1980 conference commented that in the minds of many people open admissions in higher education is a dead issue. He went on to assert that "open admissions is a con game" because after being admitted students often cannot get into the program they want to be in. These comments generated lively discussion among the participants, with most soundly rejecting them. One participant pointed out that being admitted to an institution (getting in the door) never guarantees being admitted to a particular program. Another stressed that open admissions only assures the right of *access* to higher education. Whether students are then able to enter a particular program depends upon many factors, including educational background and preparedness. Students admitted through open admissions soon learn they cannot automatically become a nurse or computer programmer, for example. But they also learn that they *are able to learn* and that they may aspire to occupations that they might never have considered before.

The debate about open admissions occurred in the context of a larger discussion about the need for faculty reeducation in urban-oriented institutions and in particular about the faculty development project funded by the Ford Foundation at Jersey City State College. William Maxwell, president of Jersey City State, argued along the following lines:

As an entrance policy, open admissions is not a con game. But it can become one if the institutions and their faculties fail to understand the students and their needs. It can become one when faculty insist on traditional approaches where flexibility is called for, when the quality of education is lowered because the students are somehow regarded as less worthy or able, or when the institutions fail to make sure that students know what is expected of them and what they must be prepared to do if they are to succeed in college or to work successfully in a field that interests them.

Maxwell's main point was that students are entitled to know whether particular institutions have the capacity and the will to serve their needs effectively. A good many institutions do not and are not truthful about it. To the extent that they are not truthful, the students are cheated by policies of open admissions that promise, in effect, more than the institutions can deliver.

Important issues are imbedded in such comments about open admissions. In this paper we can do little more than flag them for the reader's attention. Nevertheless, it is clear that the concept of open admissions is far from a dead issue. Although it has undergone changes in recent years—some good, some bad—and although some people may wish it would go away, open admissions and the social and educational values it embraces will remain an important issue for the future.

Basic Skills and
Related Programs and Services

The single greatest problem facing urban-oriented colleges and universities today is the urgent need of their students and potential students for help with basic skills. Not only do existing programs in the institutions need to be strengthened and expanded—and attitudes about the programs and the students changed—but also imaginative and unconventional approaches are needed in recruitment, testing, placement, counseling, and guidance. Even the teaching of basic skills themselves must be restructured. No less importantly, information about basic skills and related programs must be made more widely available, and in a form that will reach the inner-city poor and disadvantaged.

Broadly speaking, two populations should be the target of such efforts. One is made up of students in college who are having learning difficulties and whose problems are reflected most dramatically in high attrition rates. The other is made up of young people and adults—at work, in unemployment lines, on the streets, or even in the schools—who want and need further education but are discouraged from pursuing it because of their deficiencies in basic skills or accumulated frustrations from past learning failures. Both groups are diverse and ever changing; both present difficult challenges for educational institutions. The projects discussed below show the many ways urban-oriented institutions of higher education in six different city contexts are attempting to come to grips with the learning problems of these groups.

IN-SCHOOL YOUTH: MILES COLLEGE AND
THE BIRMINGHAM SCHOOLS COOPERATE

In race relations, Birmingham, Alabama, has come a long way from the turmoil of the 1960s. Today it is a relatively peaceful city whose

19

black citizens occupy positions of power and leadership in almost every phase of community life.

Birmingham has a population of more than 300,000, of whom 42 percent are black. Although heavy industry (mainly steel) is still important, the economy is increasingly dependent on service industries, which tend to require a better-educated, more skilled work force. Like other cities, Birmingham is also afflicted with urban blight, poverty, and unemployment (especially among blacks), white flight (and related urban-suburban conflict), a high crime rate, and a public school system that has failed to educate black youth. Failure of the school system is cited by local leaders as the city's most alarming problem.

According to the Birmingham Chamber of Commerce, the majority of high school graduates as well as dropouts leave school with no more than an eighth-grade proficiency in reading, writing, spelling, and mathematics. Most are not even able to fill out an application for employment. Under a recent mandate from the Board of Education, the schools have begun to draw up plans to address the problems and to submit the plans in writing for the board's approval. But putting the plans into action will be long and arduous.

This is the situation that Birmingham's Miles College chose to address. A small, relatively poor, predominantly black college, Miles has far fewer resources and only half as many black students as the University of Alabama at Birmingham. Yet it has been the avenue to higher education for thousands of poor and educationally disadvantaged black youngsters in Birmingham who simply would not have succeeded in college without the special attention and support that Miles is designed to give them. It is, by mission and history, a symbol of hope for the most severely disadvantaged, and it is held in high regard by the city.

Miles College has a clear sense of its own mission. It recognizes that if the real needs of Birmingham's poor and disadvantaged are to be met, it must be prepared to operate in flexible and creative ways. That kind of thinking has led the college to initiate collaborative efforts with the city's public schools over the years. As a result, Miles has a strong track record in providing basic skills training for area high school students and dropouts.

Despite the efforts of Miles College and other Birmingham institutions to work with in-school and out-of-school youth on basic skills, data from national achievement tests show that by the time Birmingham students reach senior high school, they are two to three years behind in skills proficiency. This problem is not peculiar to Birmingham, of course—it is a fact of life for the great majority of inner-city school systems throughout the country. Miles College concluded that intervention was needed much earlier in the students' careers if the problem was to be addressed at its core. In one of the projects funded by the Ford Foundation, an experiment was carried out by Miles to do just that.

In the fall of 1978, Miles's Skills Upgrading Program for Educational Reinforcement (SUPER) began a program of counseling and tutoring in basic skills for elementary and early secondary school students. The main elements were: diagnostic testing and development of student profiles; one-on-one and group tutoring (in reading, writing, spelling, and mathematics); workshops for tutors, teachers, parents, guidance counselors, and principals in which they exchanged information and planning ideas; and tutors' visits to the students' teachers in the schools and to their parents at home. The teaching program was reinforced by other activities. For example, films and lectures were presented on drug abuse, sex education, and problems of urban street life that face youth daily and affect their learning. And group trips were arranged to points of interest and cultural events in the city.

SUPER operated after school hours, in four tutorial sites—set up on the Miles campus and in two high schools and in an elementary school in severely depressed, predominantly black neighborhoods of Birmingham. Over 500 students were served by the program during the two-year experimental phase. The focus was on students with basic skills far below grade level, poor attendance records, and low participation in school activities, and on those who had been held back at various grade levels resulting in age-difference problems with their classmates—in short, students most likely to drop out of school because of a strong sense of failure. Guidance counselors, principals, and classroom teachers worked with the tutors to select students from the SUPER program, and parent approval was required for the students' participation.

At the different sites the program was staffed by a total of nineteen part-time retired teachers from the black community, each of whom was experienced in teaching basic skills to disadvantaged youngsters. The tutors, both male and female, ranged in age from fifty-one to seventy-nine. All had bachelor's degrees. Some had done some graduate work, but having an advanced degree was considered less important than experience, commitment, and understanding.

The retired teachers were hired part-time by the full-time SUPER project director, herself a retired teacher and a graduate of Miles. She was widely known and respected in the city for her innovative approach to teaching and involvement in community affairs. The director was selected by W. Clyde Williams, president of Miles College, in consultation with other college officials, community and government leaders, and the schools. Indeed, the project had considerable community participation in the form of an advisory committee whose membership was drawn from the schools, parent and student associations, citizen-participation and planning groups, and city government.

The SUPER program was monitored by Foundation staff and consultants, including James R. Jordan of the American Council on Education, who reported on the project in detail after two years of operation. He looked especially for evidence that the students exposed to the program had advanced measurably in basic skills proficiency. SUPER sought to lift each student's mastery of basic skills by two grade levels. To measure their progress, the California Achievement Test was administered for pre-testing and post-testing purposes. In purely quantitative terms, analysis of the test scores revealed gains in mean grade scores, particularly for the younger students. First-graders in the program performed at the first-grade level on the post-test. The mean grade equivalent score for second-graders in the program was 2.5. For third-graders, it was 3.1. For children in fourth, fifth, and sixth grades the scores were 3.6, 5.1, and 5.9, respectively. For seventh- and eighth-graders, the scores were 5.5 and 5.4.[5]

These figures reflect group tendencies at each grade level; thus some students at each level performed below the mean grade score, others above it. According to the data, one "second-grader performed at very nearly the fifth-grade level, one third-grader exceeded the fifth-grade level, a fourth-grader reached a level of seven months into the sixth grade, several fifth-graders performed several months above the seventh grade, and four sixth-graders exceeded the ninth-grade level, one exceeding the twelfth-grade standard and another that of the tenth grade."[6]

The data show that despite progress in basic skills, students in grades seven and eight were still performing well below grade level (while in grades three to six the performance was more or less *at* grade level). In assessing this result, those involved in the testing and score analysis at Miles stressed that the two upper grade levels "must be considered in the light of the fact that the level of difficulty of the material to be learned increased in direct proportion to the grade level. Achieving successively higher grade levels is more difficult for those who have fallen behind in the earlier grades, because the learning deficit is cumulative."[7] Nevertheless, even at these levels the students did make significant quantitative gains.

The results of the SUPER program are impressive by any standard;

they speak for themselves. For the purposes of this paper, the points to be stressed about the program and its success are as follows:

- Persons at all levels of the Birmingham community recognized the problem and committed themselves to do something about it.

- Miles College understood its mission and its interdependency with the community.

- The president of the college had a strong personal commitment to the program, as well as good working relations with the local superintendent of schools and the governor of Alabama, who was himself concerned about illiteracy in the schools throughout the state.

- Teachers, tutors, and parents were eager to cooperate, and the program was designed to facilitate their interaction.

- The college had a good track record of providing basic skills at the high school level, and both the college and the retired teachers who participated knew from experience what was needed by way of curriculum, instructional format, and nonacademic reinforcement.

- The tutors were black, a factor of some importance to the black youngsters making up most of the enrollment.

- The program included a pre-testing and a post-testing phase to measure the quantitative gains made by SUPER students.

- The use of retired teachers from the community, who were experienced in basic skills training for disadvantaged youngsters, was essential. Regular classroom teachers were already overburdened, and regular classroom approaches were ill-suited to the special needs of disadvantaged learners. But the cooperation of the regular school teachers was essential.

- The retired teachers, all committed professionals, were turned loose to do what they knew was needed, both in the details of teaching and in providing a kind of parenting or special support for students who needed emotional reinforcement.

By using retired people, it was possible for the project to keep salary costs to a minimum. In each of the two years of the experimental phase, the budget provided only $20,000 for the full-time director and her staff. An additional $20,000 was provided for the salaries of the part-time tutors. James Jordan calculated an overall per-student cost for the project of about $320, noting that the program was an educational bargain. For the tutors, even modest compensation for their services was an important supplement to their fixed incomes as retirees. And most of them welcomed the opportunity to become productive members of society again.

We have discussed the SUPER program in the past tense because it has been in abeyance while the college documents the experience, develops refinements for the future, and shares the model with others around the state. In the judgment of the president of Miles, the program will be needed in Birmingham for at least another decade; and funding for its continuation from local and state sources seems assured.

FACULTY DEVELOPMENT: THE JERSEY CITY CASE

At least four forces work against effective basic skills training at the college level, even when courses in basic skills are offered. First, many faculty members and administrators judge such courses to be inappropriate in a college or university, or at best peripheral. Second, because the courses are deemed "subcollegiate," they usually carry no academic credit. In effect, students are penalized for their past failures. Third, faculty (and sometimes the administration) do not understand the educational needs of disadvantaged people in the larger community, especially their need for basic skills training as a preliminary for regular college work. Fourth, faculty members who do recognize the need for basic skills courses are seldom trained to teach them, and in any case are inclined to resist getting involved in such "lesser" activities. Senior faculty (usually tenured) tend to relegate the job to junior faculty (usually untenured) or to special basic skills faculty.

One result of these attitudes and practices is that even after students "complete" basic skills training many are unable to perform well in regular courses. Help with basic skills at the point of entry is not enough; they need reinforcement on a continuing basis, but it is seldom available as an integrated, on-going part of their studies. Having been isolated in entry-level basic skills courses on the periphery of the institution, they have difficulty relating the learning of basic skills to the content of core courses. Unable to perform well, they give up and drop out.

In the view of many institutional leaders, including the president of Jersey City State College, the solution to this problem is to modify the regular curriculum so that training in basic skills is woven into core courses. To do that, substantial work with existing faculty is essen-

24

tial, since funds for new personnel are now scarce and will continue to be so. The project at Jersey City State College addressed these propositions.

Hudson County, New Jersey, is a forty-one-square-mile peninsula just across the Hudson River from New York City. Its population of 610,000 is the poorest and least well-educated of any urban county in New Jersey, and it has the highest percentage of foreign-born of any county in the United States. Jersey City, with a population of about 260,000, is Hudson County's geographic and governmental center.

Since the end of European immigration at the close of World War I, three waves of immigrants have moved across Hudson County: blacks from the rural South between the end of World War II and 1965; Cubans and Puerto Ricans from 1950 on; and, in recent years, Egyptians, Koreans, Greeks, Vietnamese, Indians, and South Americans have poured into Jersey City. Because immigrant groups have tended to cluster in well-defined geographic areas of the county, educational services can be fairly easily tailored to their needs. Besides these shifts in population, Jersey City suffers from the usual urban problems—high unemployment, a high crime rate, and neighborhood deterioration.

The Hudson County–Jersey City area is the only urban area of the state with a cluster of colleges and universities intended primarily to serve the region's urban population, including the local poor and disadvantaged. Three are in Jersey City and the fourth, Stevens Institute of Technology, is in adjacent Hoboken.

Stevens serves students well-prepared for its engineering program and able to benefit from traditional modes of instruction. Saint Peter's College has traditionally served white, middle-class working adults, but, as a result of recent population changes, it is moving toward greater service to disadvantaged minority and ethnic groups. Jersey City State College and Hudson County Community College have relatively open admissions and a strong history of services to the area's economically and educationally disadvantaged. Jersey City State is by far the largest of the area's institutions, with an annual enrollment of some 10,000 students. It therefore has special importance to the city and its disadvantaged residents.

Because of their strong orientation to local needs, three of the institutions took part in the Foundation's faculty development project: Jersey City State, Saint Peter's, and Hudson County Community. Jersey City State was the grant recipient, and it assumed responsibility for the project's development and implementation. (Nearly 80 percent of its students enter college in serious need of help with basic skills and language training; 85 percent of its faculty is tenured.)

All three institutions offer a variety of basic skills courses in reading, writing, mathematics, and English. Over the years, the courses have been revised several times. Originally they were set up as add-ons to regular courses, but officials came to believe that basic skills training should be worked into the regular curricula, particularly in general studies and introductory-level courses. It had become obvious that students master basic skills most effectively when they are reinforced in regular learning situations.

The project strategy was for basic skills faculty and instructional designers in the institutions to work with core faculty from different disciplines. Through workshops, informal faculty meetings, and development of teaching materials, the project aimed to help the faculty become sensitive to the needs and problems of the special kinds of students they serve, expose them to new and varied teaching methods in basic skills, and assist them in revising their curriculum and teaching approaches to include basic skills. The goal was to modify the teaching approaches and the structure and content of approximately forty core courses by the end of two years.

Each of the three institutions set up a faculty service center on its campus for the duration of the project. Each center had a director and was staffed by faculty advisers in reading, writing, mathematics, and bilingual education, and by clerical help—all working on released time from their regular college jobs. The director of the Jersey City State College center, who served as overall project director, was the only full-time employee of the project. The project directors met regularly to coordinate and promote the activities of their centers. One activity was the development of extended profiles for each student, including academic evaluations (high school transcripts, test scores), information about age, ethnic background, financial circumstance, employment, if any, and the student's own perception of his or her situation and expectations. An academic history of each student was maintained. (Students had access to their files, as did their teachers.)

In addition to building and maintaining student profiles, the centers held informal meetings and formal workshops, some for the entire faculty and others for faculty participating directly in the project. Some workshops were cross-departmental within an institution, and some were interinstitutional. They had various purposes: to examine curricular matters and modes of instruction; to make the faculty sensitive to the special language needs of new immigrant students; to develop practical ways of helping students with poor basic skills; and to investigate ways to reinforce skills and improve counseling and testing. Center directors and basic skills faculty served as advisers; outside consultants were hired when needed.

26

There also were efforts to reach beyond the institution in other ways. At Jersey City State College, which has close ties with the local school system, adjunct workshops were held for public school teachers and those involved in their training. The purpose was to learn teachers' perceptions of student needs and how to meet them in the classroom. The college, which has major responsibility for preparing teachers in Hudson County, hoped to improve its teacher-training programs as a result of the exchange.

Not surprisingly, the goal of modifying forty courses in two years was not reached. Faculty attitudes and teaching behavior are ordinarily very difficult to change—a problem compounded by the tenure system, unionization, and compartmentalization of subject matter into narrow and well-defined areas of specialization. Both the Foundation and the institutions recognized at the outset that progress would be slow toward the desired goal and went into the effort with a guarded optimism and a willingness to accept small incremental gains.

By the time the experimental phase of the project ended in mid-1980, several monitoring visits had been made. Talks with a wide range of people revealed that the effort produced several important results. In all three institutions some curriculum revision *did* occur. New materials were developed and used in several courses. The core faculty involved in workshops, in meetings, and in revising courses showed a clearer understanding of how to improve students' basic skills. And in each institution faculty attitudes had changed for the better.

As a result of its participation in the project, Saint Peter's College has since moved to create a permanent Faculty Service Center on its campus, funded from regular institutional budgets and Title III funds. Hudson County Community College, which had no faculty of its own at the time of the grant (it contracted to other institutions for faculty), has hired two dozen basic skills faculty to work with the core faculty it is now building. The college can afford to take on so many faculty for basic skills because it is funded by the county under a formula that assures a certain level of state funding.

Concrete change was more difficult to measure at Jersey City State College because it is larger and more complex, but in conversations with faculty and administrators there we found a high degree of continuing interest in the project. It had clearly demonstrated to them what could be done. Unfortunately, the college's total reliance on state funding gives it little budget flexibility, and in a time of economic austerity it could not continue the work on its own. Without further outside help, the project would necessarily have been terminated after two years. Thus, the Foundation made a supplemental two-year grant in mid-1980. Matched one to one by in-kind contributions from the college, these resources are being used to establish at Jersey City State a permanent faculty service and development facility—the Center for Innovative Teaching. Located in the School of Arts and Sciences and administered by the school's Director of General Studies and Assistant Dean, the center aims to offer a visible place for faculty to get help in redesigning courses. The Jersey City experience suggests that where faculty are willing and institutional leadership is committed, faculty development around basic skills can take place, however slowly. Moreover, the effort itself is a bread-and-butter program that can be duplicated almost anywhere.

At the Ford Foundation conference (May 1980), two sets of comments emerged in discussions about faculty development, basic skills, and the Jersey City experience. They are worth reporting here.

The president of Jersey City State College, William Maxwell, noted that although there was success in all areas of the project, it was often a case of the converted talking with the converted. He said that his college tried to persuade all faculty to join in the effort but it did not compel them to do so. He insisted that in any faculty development effort it is important to recognize three realities: the way college faculties (or school teachers for that matter) expect to live out their professional lives; the way they are actually doing that; and the way the institution is trying to make them change. He said that though we bemoan the tendency of faculty to resist change, we should remember that they are not so different from the rest of us. He went on to reaffirm his commitment to continue faculty development within Jersey City State, but noted that he was also pessimistic. He said he doubted that even the best efforts can reach the majority of faculty, and that urban-oriented colleges and universities, despite programs of this sort, will be unable to make dramatic changes in basic skills programs without a substantial infusion of new funds. We found this theme of insufficient funding echoed by officials of urban-oriented institutions of higher education all across the country.

Another conference participant, Roger Yarrington of the American Association of Junior and Community Colleges, observed that alternatives to faculty development, especially approaches that produce quicker results, should be explored. Examples of how this might be done, he said, are contained in a report made to the President's National Advisory Council on Education in 1972.* In any case, he went

*The report, "People for the People's Colleges," by Terry O'Banion, was published by the University of Arizona Press under the title *Teachers for Tomorrow* (1972).

on, existing alternatives should be identified and the more promising of them made more widely known.

Mr. Yarrington further said that if efforts are to go forward to provide basic skills on a level commensurate with the need, accurate data are essential. As it is now, very little is known about the numbers of people who need help with basic skills. These numbers affect funding and are important to inform policy. For example, state legislatures and planning boards must know what institutions are being asked to do to improve basic skills, how many persons are being served, how many are not, and what the characteristics of both groups are. They also need to know who the teachers are, their backgrounds and their preparation. Most importantly, all concerned parties need a clearer grasp of how present programs and services are being paid for.

In concluding this section on faculty development, let us make a few general observations. If college teachers are to be called upon increasingly to help improve students' basic skills, they should be given professional recognition for their efforts. This is a familiar refrain, yet the publish-or-perish syndrome persists. Research and scholarship undertaken to advance knowledge are generally valued more highly than innovative curricula and teaching methods that faculty members devise to benefit their own students and institutions. Frank Bonilla, a professor of political science and director of the Center for Puerto Rican Studies of the City University of New York, speaks compellingly of this problem from firsthand experience. In a letter to the Ford Foundation about its grant program, he said:

> What minority people in urban settings seek desperately from education, in addition to basic intellectual and social skills, is a sense of efficacy, an ability to understand the work, to imagine and advance toward some desirable future state of the society in which they have a self-defined and valued place . . . Major universities and the scientific establishment will not respond to those needs; urban-oriented universities may be able to do so under certain conditions. These conditions were present a few years ago, retain considerable potential, but have also been dissipated by cutbacks, confusion, loss of hope, opportunism, and the hostility of those who always saw ventures in this direction as a diversion from the true goals of "higher" education. *I still receive commiserating remarks from former colleagues who are convinced that I have sacrificed a career of real scholarship to labor in the confines of an ethnically delimited, anti-intellectual and heavily ideologized ghetto.* Overcoming these stereotypes, assembling the necessary resources and talents . . . are all part of what remains to be done.   (Emphasis added)

Of course, one of the greatest rewards to faculty for participating in basic skills instruction, indeed for taking part in innovative teaching generally, is the personal satisfaction they derive from it. Faculty members who see students improving are often eager to continue working on their behalf, but the incentive of professional recognition for their efforts is lacking, and they tend to retreat eventually into accepted practice. It is worth noting that senior faculty members at Jersey City State College who were involved in developing basic skills methodology and content for their own courses continued to do so on a voluntary basis when the pilot phase of the project came to an end after two years and future funding was uncertain.

As suggested earlier, institutions that now complain of students' "failure to recognize the values of a college education" are not properly conveying this value to students. Students must make real financial and personal sacrifices to attend colleges that often do not define their educational mission in a meaningful way. Eventually, such failures result in lessened political support from the community and a shrinking funding base.

The development and implementation of a basic skills curriculum is costly and requires that innovative funding mechanisms be sought. At the same time, the very colleges that complain about the level of funds received for credit courses do not provide credit for basic skills courses and thus do not receive funding for them. As of mid-1981, Hudson County Community College, for one, was reassessing this practice. Its faculty are documenting evidence that basic skills courses do result in students' acquiring a level of linguistic and other skills that puts them on a par with students taking credit courses. There is no reason—perhaps other than "tradition"—that basic skills courses should be noncredit courses.

ENGLISH AS A SECOND LANGUAGE: COMMUNITY OUTREACH IN HARTFORD

The preceding discussion focused on the basic skills problems of in-school youth and adults already in college. But there are literally hundreds of thousands of unemployed youths, high school dropouts, marginally employed immigrants, and others not served by the educational establishment, all of whom need the benefits of higher education to improve their employment prospects. A third Foundation project was addressed to Hispanics in Hartford, Connecticut, whose native language is not English.

In Hartford, as in many other cities, Hispanics are the fastest-growing segment of the population. Yet their rate of participation in employment and in higher education remains disproportionately low. One reason is their need for help with English and other basic skills. Yet even when local institutions have the necessary instructional programs, those who need them most often do not know about them or lack the motivation to seek them out. It is then incumbent upon the institutions to mount community outreach and recruitment efforts that provide information, guidance and counseling, and instruction geared to unconventional needs, both academic and psychological. That is what the Hartford Higher Education Hispanic (HHEH) program is all about.* The general setting from which the program emerged is described below:

> The greater Hartford area has a population of about 800,000, of which some 140,000 live in the city of Hartford. Hartford is troubled by the same problems as many of its larger urban counterparts: for example, a changing population; outmigration of middle-income people to the suburbs; change in the labor structure owing to the loss in recent years of manufacturing jobs; and deterioration of municipal services. The current population of Hartford is about two-thirds minority and one-third white. Adjusted 1970 census data indicate that blacks are currently stabilized at about 30 percent of the Hartford population. Hispanics made up 8 percent of the population in 1970, but their numbers have grown very rapidly in the past decade. Current estimates for Hispanics range from 20 to 35 percent of the population. School enrollment, as based on actual headcount data collected annually by the Hartford school board, showed that Hispanics—the majority of them Puerto Rican—accounted for about 36 percent of the public school enrollment in 1979, up from 33 percent only a year before. (Blacks accounted for about 47 percent.) That is four times the percentage of only a decade ago, and there is every sign of continuing growth both in Hispanic school enrollment and the Hispanic population generally.
>
> Federal census data indicate that in 1975 the median income of Hispanics in Connecticut was $8,462, about half that of the general population. Some 60 percent of Hispanics (and only a slightly lesser percentage of blacks) were classified as below the poverty level in the state. Although state and local data on income are not available in very useful or up-to-date form, federal data are current. They indicate generally that the great majority of Hispanics are concentrated in the inner cities, both nationally and in the State of Connecticut. Very probably their numbers relative to the

*A full discussion of the project and its results appears in *A Tale of Three Cities: Boston, Birmingham, Hartford* (New York: Ford Foundation, 1981), pp. 53–72.

Hartford population are even larger than those shown above. There has been so much volatility in unemployment rates and in Hispanic migration and immigration patterns over the last few years that there is at present considerable disagreement in Hartford and in the state about the unemployment rate of Hartford Hispanics. Connecticut's Department of Labor places it at around 18 percent (as contrasted to 10 percent–12 percent for the city as a whole), but Hispanic community groups in Hartford estimate the rate to be as high as 30 percent to 40 percent for Hispanics generally and even higher for Hispanic youth. However imprecise the data, it seems clear that Hispanics in Hartford are disproportionately impoverished and unemployed.

In any case, there is no doubt about the dramatic change in the makeup of Hartford's public school enrollment (from 48 percent minority in 1965 to 85 percent now). The change has occurred so swiftly that the school system has been unable to shift gears quickly enough to meet the new demands placed upon it. As a result, large numbers of students (particularly Hispanics) drop out or graduate without adequate skills. According to the local school board, 90 percent of Hispanic high school students in Hartford drop out. In short, the odds are overwhelmingly against a Hispanic going to college.

Even for Hispanic high school students who do graduate, the probability of attending college is low. In 1974 only 81 Hispanic students were in attendance in Hartford's three largest institutions of higher education . . . and more than a third of the students were not from the Hartford area. By early 1979, the situation had improved only slightly. Fewer than 200 Hispanics were then enrolled in the three institutions. Ninety were at the University of Hartford, four at Hartford State Technical College, and the rest at the Greater Hartford Community College.[8]

Against this background, the aforementioned institutions, two of them public and one private, joined together under the leadership of the University of Hartford (the largest of the three) to address the problem. All were concerned about their low level of service to Hispanics in the area—indeed they were under pressure from local Hispanic leaders to do something about it—and despite a history of operating in relative isolation from each other, they decided to cooperate in the Hartford Higher Education Hispanic program.

The program had four interrelated components: recruitment; testing and placement of students; group and one-on-one tutoring in basic skills and language; and guidance. Both academic and personal counseling were offered throughout the program and continued in many cases after HHEH students enrolled in college.

Recruitment took many forms: project personnel contacted future students on the streets; Hispanic community agencies, church groups, and high school counselors helped identify potential students at home and on the job; and the media announced the program. They were placed in basic skills and English courses, all offered on the university campus, at basic, intermediate, and advanced levels; some students, during the project's pilot year (the summer of 1979 through the spring of 1980), completed work at more than one level. Because of its extensive involvement in bilingual education programs in the past, the university had the methodology, diagnostic and instructional materials, and trained personnel needed for the program.

Instruction was provided by eighteen university faculty and staff working on a part-time released basis. Faculty and administrative personnel from the three institutions, including deans and the presidents, helped design the project initially and remained active in its implementation through a project steering committee and occasional meetings with the project staff and faculty. But the heart of the effort in finding and motivating potential students was in recruitment and personal counseling provided by three Hispanics, each located in an office on one of the three campuses. Two worked part-time; the one full-time person also served as overall project coordinator under the direction of the dean of the College of Education and Allied Services at the University of Hartford. We cannot stress enough how important these three were to the outcome of the project. They knew from firsthand experience the problems faced by their fellow Hispanics.

The HHEH project made impressive progress toward the goal of getting more Hispanics in the area enrolled in college. Out of ninety-three students in the project during the pilot year, fifty-two were enrolled in area colleges by the fall of 1980; as might be expected, the enrollments were concentrated in the two public institutions. Only nine students dropped out. Many of the thirty-two who completed the HHEH program but did not enroll in college were expected to do so in the future, and some have now done so. Others had no need for college study because they had been practicing professionals in their country of origin and were in the program only to improve their English.

On the evidence of the program's value to Hartford Hispanics, and its potential for replication in other urban contexts, the Ford Foundation, the Aetna Life and Casualty Foundation of Hartford, and the University of Hartford joined in funding the program's continuance through 1984. It is expected that cooperation among the university and the two public colleges will continue on an informal basis as before.

Counseling Services: Shortcomings in Current Practices. Counseling and guidance programs are essential for disadvantaged learners. The majority of students who are or should be served by urban-oriented institutions come from economically and socially unstable communities. They need counseling programs that can provide a sense of family and even, on occasion, serve a parenting function. Both the Miles College and the University of Hartford programs recognize that fundamental reality.

This is not a new role for institutions of higher education. In residential colleges and universities, dormitories and house directors provide a kind of family, a service for which the students are charged. Nonresidential urban-oriented institutions have to give their part-time nontraditional students a similar service but in less conventional ways and with less latitude in offsetting the costs. Many do a good job of it, but most do not. Because of underfunding and insensitivity to student needs, counseling services in urban-oriented institutions tend to be fragmented, overburdened, and misdirected.

Fragmented Counseling Services. Students are expected to go to one group of faculty or staff for academic counseling and to different people for personal, social, and financial counseling. Unlike those in the Hartford program, the various types of counselors are seldom in regular communication. This disjointed approach makes it difficult to provide guidance based on an understanding of the needs of the whole person. Yet the most effective counseling takes account of the whole person when addressing the problem at hand, whether that problem is academic or personal.

Counseling based on the needs of the total person has long been a hallmark of small, select colleges. Students in them tend to interact closely with faculty not only in academic pursuits but in matters of personal and social development. The faculty know the students as individuals with a variety of needs. Because the faculty live on or near the college—and have offices on campus—they are highly accessible to students and more likely to be available for informal conversations that enhance the students' sense that they are part of the college family. These faculty provide an important service, even though their students do not require so much emotional and psychological reinforcement as the disadvantaged students in urban-oriented colleges and universities.

By contrast, at urban-oriented institutions faculty often travel long distances and maintain only minimal office hours. Many do not even have regular office space available to them. These factors leave them less accessible to students, though there are exceptions. At the sprawling campus of the University of the District of Columbia, for example, students attending the undergraduate college, located in downtown Washington, receive academic counseling on the premises. But even here the students must travel to the Van Ness Campus several miles away for other kinds of counseling. One effect of this multiple counseling approach is that students are obliged first to find out that there *are* different kinds of counselors and then to seek the kind best suited to the problem at hand. It demands a sophistication not needed by students at traditional residential institutions where coordinated counseling is built into studying and living arrangements. Another effect is that counseling services in many urban-oriented institutions are underused, leaving administrators and policy makers with inaccurate information about the need for such services among the students. Unfortunately, underuse by students is too often taken as evidence that need does not exist. The funding implications are obvious.

Overburdened Staffs. In many institutions, largely for reasons of underfunding, counseling staffs are overburdened. A survey conducted by the Washington Office of the College Board in 1979 found that the ratios of students to counselors are significantly higher in inner-city schools than in schools outside the city.[9] There is good reason to believe that the same situation exists in urban-oriented institutions of higher education. At the Hartford State Technical College, "state funds pay for only one counselor for the college's entire student body and [that] counselor is also the financial aid officer."[10] It is noteworthy that the recruiter-counselors, who have such central importance to the Hartford project, were newly hired and paid out of external funds.

Conventional Responses. Traditional counseling is designed to meet the needs of conventional four-year students headed for graduate study. Many students in urban-oriented institutions will probably not go to graduate school; some are not even working toward a four-year degree. They are interested in finding good jobs and need counseling toward that immediate end. To provide job-oriented counseling, the counselors need to be in close contact with business and industry and even to be able to direct students to the personnel offices of places of employment. Northeastern University in Boston and CUNY's La Guardia Community College in New York provide this kind of counseling very effectively through their cooperative education programs, but most urban institutions are not nearly as active in this area as they should be and as the needs of their students require.

DIAGNOSTIC TESTING:
STRATEGIES IN THE DISTRICT OF COLUMBIA

Standardized testing in American society has been used largely to exclude or screen out. Diagnostic testing is more creative. It aims to help students overcome their learning deficiencies by diagnosing their strengths and weaknesses as a preliminary to placing them in instructional programs geared to their needs, as well as to provide a benchmark against which to measure progress. Most urban-oriented institutions use some form of testing for diagnostic and prescriptive purposes, but how effectively or extensively they do so is open to question. Many try to use standardized tests in ways for which they were not designed. Others try to use diagnostic tools that have evolved out of the recent open-learning movement but are still in the developmental stage. Organizations such as the Council for the Advancement of Experiential Learning have been working to develop practical instruments of diagnostic testing and to help colleges and universities adapt them to local circumstances. Because these efforts are underfunded, they are advancing slowly. They are unlikely to pick up speed without more generous funding by federal and foundation sources; unfortunately, those who control the purse strings still tend to be skeptical of such work.

Of course, not all urban-oriented institutions fully recognize the significance of diagnostic testing for their efforts to serve disadvantaged learners. The University of the District of Columbia does. It sees the planning and development of a comprehensive testing program as a key element in reducing student attrition—for without it, effective counseling, guidance, and instruction simply cannot be provided. A Foundation grant in 1978 aimed to help the university develop such a program.

To put this effort in perspective, let us consider briefly the context in which the university operates. Thirty years ago Washington, D.C., had a predominantly white, middle-class, well-educated population, the majority of whom worked for the federal government. Today, 70 percent of the district's population of over 637,000 is black. The majority are underschooled, underemployed, and socially, economically, and educationally locked in. The district also has a growing community of Hispanic immigrants from some twenty nations, most of whom are very poor.

The District of Columbia has seventeen institutions of higher education. Eleven are small, church-related, or special-purpose colleges with enrollments of a few hundred each. Five, including Howard University, are large, private, national/international institutions.

Only the University of the District of Columbia, a public institution, was created specifically to serve the educational needs of inner-city residents. Its enrollment is about 10,000; its predominantly black students are, in general, poor, disadvantaged, and in need of extensive help with learning skills.

The university is the result of a merger of three public institutions in 1976—Teachers College of the District of Columbia (established in 1800), Washington Technical Institute, and Federal City College (the latter two established in the 1960s). Unlike the other institutions discussed in this paper, the University of the District of Columbia is, in a sense, a developing institution, one that is trying to build supply and demand at the same time. Thus, the Foundation viewed its grant more as a way to help the university enhance its own well-defined mission than as encouragement to develop a model that might be followed by other urban-oriented institutions. At this writing, less is known about concrete change at the university as a result of the project than about the work being undertaken and the process by which it is being pursued. The following are the main project activities:

- Each of the university's predecessor institutions had some form of diagnostic and developmental testing. The various elements of their programs are now being merged into a single, integrated program based in the University College, which was created by the university primarily to deal with attrition problems; the college provides an array of instructional, support, and research services.

- The testing staffs from the three earlier institutions now form a temporary working group to plan modifications in procedure, testing approaches, counseling, and academic service. The overall director of this effort is the dean of University College. A full-time coordinator, who handles day-to-day management, is experienced in developmental/diagnostic testing, traditional and nontraditional modes of instruction, and evaluation.

- To ensure participation by faculty and staff, and as a demonstration of his own commitment to the effort, the president of the university has appointed several faculty and staff to a program development team. They are specialists in reading, mathematics, English, language arts, basic skills, and diagnostic-prescriptive learning; they consult regularly with the working groups of testing staff from the predecessor institutions.

- Plans are under way to cooperate more closely with the public school system in the district, to develop mechanisms geared to assessing the needs of older students, to perform pilot testing on students from the college and from local high schools, to devise the use of alternate testing and assessment methods, and to analyze cost factors associated with each.

- Staff development sessions are being held to familiarize faculty with the uses of testing data and new approaches to curriculum development and improvement of teaching techniques.

- Efforts are under way to develop "analytic transcripts" that will provide academic and personal profiles of entering students. They will be used to guide the university's diagnostic, educational, and psychological counseling. They will also serve as a tool by which faculty can design instructional programs and by which students can follow their own programs.

Although these activities are a proper and necessary line of work for the university—as indeed they would be for most urban-oriented institutions of higher education—dramatic results will not be achieved overnight. But they will never be attained unless an institution has a long-term, high-level commitment to persist—as best it can in the face of budgetary constraints—along the general course described above.

Institutional Planning and Cooperation

Developing new approaches to planning should be a first order of business for urban-oriented institutions of higher education. Because many of them do not seem to understand their interdependency with the city and its people, they wind up with distorted planning and inappropriate use of resources. They also find themselves unable to articulate their institutional mission clearly or persuasively. These failures lead to others. The institutions are not only unable to produce the educational programs and services needed by the disadvantaged learner, they are also unable to acquire funding.

A good planning program should have at least five elements: (1) clear identification of disadvantaged groups that are either already served by the institution or need access to it; (2) systematic, on-going assessment of their educational needs; (3) examination of existing programs to determine their usefulness to students, and to reshape them where necessary; (4) recognition that the untraditional needs of the students require unconventional and creative responses; and (5) the gathering of information on local job-market realities. Moreover, the planning should be comprehensive—related to the total institutional context on the one hand and to the larger city context on the other.

Even with new kinds of planning, however, it is essential for the institutions, and for those who judge their performance, to recognize that they have limited resources. They cannot be all things to all people. In the first flush of open admissions and with the abundance of federal funds for higher education in the 1960s, urban-oriented colleges and universities seemed willing to serve everyone; they altered admissions standards and established ambitious new programs toward that end. Some of these programs have since been terminated because they lacked focus; others, which were working well, have been either cut out or cut back as federal funding has been reduced.

Proper institutional planning will help the institutions to understand just how much they can do. It also will help them to spot the weaknesses in their offerings and to make the benefits of cooperation more apparent. If the goal is to improve performance and outreach generally, and if that goal is agreed on, cooperation with other institutions will enable them to do far more for more people than would be possible if the institutions persisted in going it alone.

In some settings, cooperation should probably take the form of formal consortia. True, recent history is filled with failed or uninspired consortia, but institutions that join together around specific, common educational problems and objectives are more apt to produce results than those that join together primarily to attract funding.

A SIMPLE NEED FOR INFORMATION

An essential component of the interrelated programs and services discussed in this paper is the simple provision of information. Potential students need to know all kinds of things—where and how to enroll, what courses to take, where to obtain financial aid, how to apply for scholarships and loans. Lack of information may be the single greatest obstacle to attracting students.

It is a paradox of modern society that as information multiplies at every level of life, it is often not accessible to those who need it most. The poor and disadvantaged—who have historically looked upon social institutions with confusion if not dismay—find the world outside their immediate environments less and less understandable. They are intimidated, and what they see in the larger universe of the city usually seems unrelated to their needs and circumstances.

A 1977 report by La Casa de Puerto Rico,[11] a Hartford-based advocacy and research organization, found that some 67 percent of Puerto Rican high school graduates in Connecticut were either unaware of higher education services and programs available to them or needed help in identifying institutions and programs suited to their needs. The lack of financial aid remains a major barrier to the participation of Hispanics in higher education, partly because potential students do not know they are eligible for it or do not know how to apply for it. A recent College Board study reached the same conclusion (see pp. 58–63).

Increasingly, urban-oriented institutions will be obliged to solve this informational problem if they are to make higher education available to the disadvantaged of the inner city. The University of Hartford project is attempting to solve it on behalf of the Hispanics in the area through recruiting and on-campus activity that is largely informational in nature. In the case of Miles College, information is given to parents—whose cooperation, understanding, and approval is necessary for their children to take part and succeed in the SUPER program. In both instances, the project staff know exactly what information is needed, and they make sure it is communicated by sending "information messengers" into the community.

A COMPLEX NEED FOR PLANNING

Another aspect of the information problem is that many urban-oriented institutions do not collect data they need to support purposeful planning and program development. They do not, for example, regularly assess student and community needs, and they do not evaluate credit and entry-level skills courses with the same attention they give to traditional credit courses. Basic skills and related programs and services are usually understaffed, and there are simply too few people to gather information and keep detailed records, let alone to analyze them for larger institutional purposes.

Another constraint on gathering data is that part-time students, whom the institutions serve so heavily, are harder to track. Furthermore, in most institutions the problem is compounded by the phenomenon of students dropping in for several courses and then dropping out for one or more terms. Urban-oriented institutions are often criticized by education and government officials because of the high noncompletion rates resulting from this practice of dropping in and out. The truth is that neither the institutions nor outside observers really know what the phenomenon means.

What should be understood is that many students attend urban-oriented colleges and universities only long enough to upgrade skills for economic advancement; they are not after a degree. Recent studies show that less than half of the entering freshmen at two-year colleges plan to get a degree; the majority simply want to get a job, or a better job.

For those who do hope to complete all degree requirements, many have to pursue their studies over several years (sometimes in more than one institution), with interruptions for economic and personal reasons. Lisle Carter, president of the University of the District of Columbia, says that at his and other institutions, many students take eight or nine years to earn a bachelor's degree because they must work part-time. Yet institutional failure to accept this basic fact is widespread and leads to the use of teachers and support systems that are counterproductive to learning. It also leads to state and federal policies that do not fit the realities. For example, at the University of the District of Columbia, it is a common practice for students to over-load themselves with courses in order to qualify for financial aid. The connection between this practice and attrition is obvious.

Traditionally, a college education means completing degree requirements at a given institution within a given period of years. Urban-oriented institutions find it difficult to put aside this unrealistic definition. As a result, the dropout phenomenon is usually assessed both by the institution and those outside it as institutional failure to retain students. The problem of attrition is acute, of course, and when seen from that perspective alone the judgment is fair. Blanket indictments, however, are objectionable: suggestions that the students are less able than "normal" students; that the programs they need are only marginally useful; that a high attrition rate and "noncompletion" are the same thing. One aspect of the solution is evident. More accurate record-keeping, coupled with continuing assessment of student needs, would help to dispel these misconceptions and enable planners and policy makers to use institutional resources in ways that are more responsive to student needs. It also would help to ensure that state budget officials have information they need when matters of funding are at issue.

Generally speaking, institutions that engage in systematic planning, mission reexamination, and data collection and analysis—in the light of their interdependency with their cities and the people who live in them—will see clearly how urgent the need is for improving their performance vis-à-vis the needs of the inner-city poor and disadvantaged. And they will come to see that the major task before them is to educate people for jobs and careers and prepare them to earn a decent living. Moreover, proper planning and assessment will make it clear that their students' needs are largely unconventional, requiring a variety of different responses. At the very least, the institutions will recognize the need to provide: curriculum flexibility so that students can complete courses in time frames that fit their circumstances; increased counseling to minimize the students' need to interrupt their studies for financial and other reasons; job-placement counseling that will help students improve their job situation while they are acquiring new skills and training; and basic skills training to correct past deficiencies. An essential starting point for institutional planning and development is to recognize once and for all that nontraditional students are not a homogeneous group with a single set of unconventional needs.

In 1979 a statewide review of the need for educational information in Oregon[12] identified five groups (large numbers of whom live in the state's inner cities) as being poorly served educationally. The groups were minorities (black, Hispanic, Native American); women returning to the job market or entering it for the first time; single mothers and recently widowed older women; the physically handicapped; and older adults, especially those approaching retirement and those with low levels of education.

The Oregon study underscored the need for differentiated educational services for each of the groups. Toward the end, the study said, it is not helpful to use such terms as "special students," "nontraditional students," or "the new student." Even the category of "poor and disadvantaged" is not very helpful when moving beyond general arguments to consider specific remedies. Yet most institutions not only fail to make clear distinctions among these groups and their needs, but also persist in treating them as if they had the ordinary needs of traditional students by using the same recruitment, counseling, and teaching. The attitude seems to be that equal treatment will result in equal access and equal success in college.

AN APPROACH TO
PLANNING AND ASSESSMENT IN SAN FRANCISCO

The kinds of information, assessment, and planning needs discussed above were central to another project in the Ford Foundation's grant program. In 1979, the San Francisco Consortium undertook a year-long research effort with several interrelated parts:

- an assessment of the higher education needs of economically and educationally disadvantaged people in San Francisco

- a cooperative self-assessment within the consortium institutions of existing programs and services for such students

- an assessment of the business and labor sectors to determine the implications of economic and business trends for educational programs

- an examination of the role the San Francisco Unified School District plays in providing educational and special services for the disadvantaged

- efforts to improve communication within and among educational institutions in the area, labor and business, and the community

The project was conducted by an independent researcher, sensitive to the needs of poor and disadvantaged people. He directed a small staff at the consortium's central office and was responsible for analyzing the data gathered and writing a final report. The project was based on a review of published studies on the subject; questionnaires; and consultations with school officials, business and industrial leaders, government representatives, consortium faculty, and others in the Bay Area. In addition, interviews were carried out with knowledgeable representatives of various community groups known to be underserved. Interestingly, although the Asian community was reportedly most eager to meet with project staff, past experience made them highly skeptical that anything would come of it.

Again, the context in which the assessment took place is important in understanding the educational needs of the city's people. In 1973, according to federal census data, San Francisco had 756,000 inhabitants, which made it the nation's fourteenth largest city. By 1979 the population had dropped to about 645,000. As in other cities, there has been a large outmigration of white, middle-income people, with consequent losses in the tax base. At the same time, there has been an influx of Soviet Jews, Hong Kong Chinese, Vietnamese refugees, Koreans, Filipinos, and Central Americans. The current population is estimated to be about 49 percent white, 16 percent black, and 35 percent Asian and other nonwhites. About 29 percent of San Francisco's Asian migrants are below the poverty level, as are 27 percent of its blacks, 14 percent of its whites, and 19 percent of its Hispanics. Many recent immigrants have difficulties with the English language. In short, San Francisco today is heavily made up of racial and ethnic minorities and financially disadvantaged whites. Most are unskilled laborers.

At the same time, the San Francisco labor market favors the skilled, educated, and financially well off. The city has gained more jobs than it has lost in the past decade, but most of the gains have been in white-collar jobs, not in manufacturing where unskilled labor can be used. Manufacturing now accounts for only 10 percent of the labor force. Moreover, nonresidents of the city hold almost half of all the available jobs.

The public schools are beset by the same kinds of teaching, administrative, and disciplinary problems as their counterparts in other cities. Plans to address these problems had just begun to show results when Proposition 13 was passed, reducing tax revenues.

At the state level there is recognition that ethnic and racial minorities and women are seriously underrepresented in the colleges and universities of California. Thus, as a result of action taken by the state legislature in 1974, institutions of higher education have been charged to improve educational opportunities for these groups and to set goals for overcoming the problem of underrepresentation. Efforts

44

to do this are being monitored by the California Postsecondary Commission. A recent report of the commission indicates that the goals set by the institutions for 1980 have not been met, and large numbers of needy people in the state and the Bay Area remain locked out of higher education.[13]

In San Francisco there are eight accredited higher educational institutions—the San Francisco Community College District, San Francisco State University, the University of San Francisco, the University of California at San Francisco, Hastings College of Law, Golden Gate University, Cogswell College, and the California College of Podiatric Medicine. These institutions, which have a combined enrollment of 127,000 students, make up the membership of the San Francisco Consortium. As might be expected, the task of serving the poor and disadvantaged falls primarily to the public institutions, especially the Community College District.

The Ford Foundation had two choices when it considered grant prospects for San Francisco: whether to invite the more urban-oriented institutions to work together in the needed assessment work, or to encourage all area institutions to join the effort as members of the consortium. The Foundation chose the latter on the assumption that all members were to some extent concerned about the problems and that all were likely to benefit from cooperating in the project. The fact that the consortium was already established was considered a big plus.

The main product of the Foundation's grant was a 200-page report published by the consortium in April 1980. The report is a scholarly, comprehensive, and persuasive analysis. More importantly, it presents an agenda for timely action by Bay Area institutions based on carefully documented evidence. After thoroughly examining community needs, labor market trends, and institutional programs and practices (in the areas of financial aid, affirmative action, recruitment, admissions, basic skills, tutoring and counseling), the consortium reached the following principal conclusions:

- Career and vocational counseling programs in secondary and higher education should be expanded. Business and labor should cooperate with the institutions toward this end.

- Remedial courses and related services should be strengthened because growing numbers, particularly young adults, are not prepared for either college or employment.

- Consortium institutions should strengthen efforts to place disadvantaged students in jobs. Business and labor should encourage such efforts.

- Career education and liberal arts programs should be more closely integrated.

- Government, the private sector, and academic institutions should develop programs for disadvantaged learners in the Bay Area.

Useful as the project report is, its impact on consortium members may be limited. As the project was nearing completion, we spoke with several consortium representatives and learned of several problems. For one thing, members of the consortium board were apparently divided at the outset about whether the project was needed. The public institutions, particularly the Community College District, strongly favored it; the private and special-purpose institutions were less enthusiastic. One board member made the telling comment that there are plenty of educational programs available for the poor and disadvantaged already and that if people in the community fail to make use of them, it is their own fault.

Another problem, in retrospect, was in hiring a project director from outside the Bay Area. Although this decision probably led to a more objective result, it also reduced the level of institutional involvement in the work. As a result, some may not see how the report's recommendations, necessarily general in nature, fit the particulars of their own situation. The institutions themselves will have to plan ways to translate the report into concrete measures for change. Whether or not this translation will occur remains to be seen.

Another problem was that the consortium—though created to promote the exchange of ideas and resources in order to make its members more responsive to urban problems—seems to have evolved into an organization convenient mainly for political and funding purposes. Although it is a useful mechanism for regular communication among the presidents who make up the board membership, the consortium today seems to function largely as a conduit for grants. This reinforces our earlier claim that consortia formed for funding purposes are not likely to produce substantive change in institutional behavior or to contribute much to improving service to the community. Planning and assessment that involve the leadership and faculty of the institutions, whether the institutions work alone or together, have a far better chance of producing results.

We hasten to add that these comments should not be taken as proof that the San Francisco consortium has no value. It is not wrong to form a consortium for funding or political advantages, but consortia formed primarily for these reasons cannot be expected to bring about substantive change in the educational policies and practices of member institutions if that is not a central reason for their existence. Moreover, when institutions join for funding and political purposes, the composition of the consortium is likely to be different from the group that would convene to solve common educational problems. Hastings College of Law and the California College of Podiatric Medicine, for example, have different legitimate interests and educational objectives than some of the other consortium members.

We turn now to a discussion of the Foundation's grant to a group of public colleges and universities in Boston known as The Boston Six.* This project, a model of genuine institutional cooperation, illustrates the benefits that separate institutions can obtain when they unite in facing common educational concerns and are willing to put student and community needs ahead of institutional prerogatives.

THE BENEFITS OF COOPERATING: THE BOSTON MODEL

Boston is the eighteenth largest city in the United States. It has a population of about 630,000, one-sixth of whom are black. Among cities with populations above 500,000, Boston is near the bottom in median household income. Forty percent of its high school students come from families receiving public assistance. Boston's current economic problems are unemployment (about 13 percent), underemployment, and limited job options caused by the lack of a major manufacturing presence in the city.

The college-going rate of graduating high school seniors is 25 percent. This low rate is attributed by officials of The Boston Six to limited family income and limited access to low-cost education. In addition, public schools in Boston, as elsewhere in the nation, have severe dropout and attendance problems. The high schools suffer from weak curricula, inadequate performance standards and counseling services, and low staff morale—caused in part by the politics and confusions of desegregation.

The private higher education sector in Boston and the immediate metropolitan area is enormous. There are two prestigious national-international institutions (Harvard University and Massachusetts Institute of Technology), several long-established regional-national institutions, and an array of small private institutions serving special-interest constituencies. In the city of Boston itself, there are twenty-three private postsecondary institutions.

*The operations of this complex cooperative effort cannot be fully captured in summary fashion. A detailed account of the project and its achievements and problems is presented in the Ford Foundation publication *A Tale of Three Cities: Boston, Birmingham, Hartford* (1981).

By contrast, public higher education is small, and most of its institutions are relatively young. It includes the University of Massachusetts at Boston, Boston State College, Massachusetts College of Art, Bunker Hill Community College, Massachusetts Bay Community College, and Roxbury Community College. These institutions, which became The Boston Six, are urban-oriented and clearly dedicated to serving the local population. Collectively, they enroll about 20,000 students annually, 82 percent of whom are city residents. The majority of their students are nontraditional, part-time, economically and educationally disadvantaged, or members of minority groups. The institutions tend to be more innovative and flexible in their educational programs than those in the private sector.

Until the Foundation's grant was awarded late in 1978, the public institutions had never attempted to work together; a volatile political climate did not seem to favor such initiatives. For the most part they were in open competition with one another for a limited pool of local students and generally ignored the fact that some 75 percent of the graduates of Boston public schools do not go on to college—to say nothing of students (some 12 percent annually) who drop out of school before graduation. The result was duplication of programs, inadequate use of available resources, confusion in the community's perception of them, and limited outreach to the neediest people. It is ironic that in the midst of such a wealth of educational institutions—twenty-nine in the city of Boston itself—there is such a lack of educational opportunity for the city's poor and disadvantaged.

The Foundation's grant provided funds for a project in which The Boston Six joined together to improve services to the local population. The timing was ideal because the grant came just as a state commission was being formed to develop plans for reorganizing the state's public higher education system. The presidents of The Boston Six recognized that only through sharing and cooperative planning could they effectively address the city's higher educational problems over the long run. They were also politically astute enough to see that such an initiative would enhance their role in the state-wide study and help assure that the special problems of urban higher education were recognized.

During the first two years, The Boston Six engaged in a wide range of planning and assessment activity in four broad areas:

- needs assessment studies carried out by special task forces made up of institutional faculty and staff and focused largely on high school students, dropouts, and undereducated adults

- analyses of the larger city context, including the present and

48

evolving labor structure, to forecast the kinds of employment for which people in Boston need to be trained

- conferences and seminars to explore nontraditional approaches to testing and assessing prior learning and to supply information about higher educational opportunities and resources available to city residents
- analyses of programs and services in the six institutions to identify areas where a combining of resources and a joint approach would improve student access, mobility and choice, and retention

The Foundation expected that the cooperative planning of The Boston Six would lead to some changes in the institutions, but it did not require that specific changes be adopted. The planning exercise was seen primarily as a necessary preliminary to making recommendations for future change. Nevertheless, unlike the San Francisco experience, as information was gathered and interaction with the community increased, institutional commitment to cooperate grew along with an eagerness for concrete action.

By mid-1980 a number of new services and programs had been introduced by The Boston Six. For example, admissions personnel had begun to make joint visitations to public schools to provide students with information about local career opportunities and programs of instruction in the six institutions. In addition, joint financial aid teams had begun visiting the schools to provide students with information and help in applying for aid. Relatedly, a financial aid "drop-in" center was set up to provide direct financial information to both students and parents, the latter through evening workshops. Also, Boston Six faculty and staff began conducting in-service training programs for youth workers and counselors in Boston's Youth Entitlement Program and other public service agencies and in local schools. Just as importantly, The Boston Six has started to provide information for adults on the radio, at jobs, in CETA workshops, and elsewhere. Finally, plans for cross registration and a common application form were under way to enhance students' choice and mobility among institutional programs.

It is interesting that four of the new activities cited are informational. Moreover, all the new efforts are nontraditional. A major goal of The Boston Six effort is to increase access to higher education for local groups that have not been reached by the member institutions. Having assessed the barriers to full participation in higher education in the early stages of their planning, they concluded that a major block was that the people they wanted to reach simply did not know what was available—in services, programs, or financial aid. Even those who did know were confused about how to make choices among the institutions, how to enroll, or how to obtain financial aid.

The institutions accepted responsibility for this communications gap, attributing it in large part to their past tendency to compete rather than to cooperate. Although none had a comprehensive set of suitable programs and services, they had previously competed to recruit students into their own institutions from the limited pool they were used to serving. None had considered whether individual institutional programs were adequate or whether student interests were best served in the long run. In addition, even when information was available, it could usually be obtained only through traditional on-campus channels, in six different places, and the poor and disadvantaged had limited or no access to these channels. As the new activities show, joint approaches were required to reach into the community.

This is only a sampling of the tangible results to emerge from the efforts of The Boston Six. Much of the solid progress made is due to an extraordinary commitment to the project by the institutional presidents, the senior vice-president for academic affairs at the University of Massachusetts (the project's principal architect and chairman of the project steering committee during the grant period), and The Boston Six project director, who continues in that position.

The institutions were not content to stop with these results. They continue to work on planning and resource sharing, and on developing stronger cooperative links with business and industry and other community agencies. Toward these ends, they committed themselves at the end of the grant period to providing nearly $100,000 annually for continued cooperation—largely through reallocating internal resources—for the next several years.

In mid-1980, five new projects were on The Boston Six agenda for future action. Whether the projects will actually materialize and on what scale is hard to predict because they will require large amounts of outside funding. We cite them here to illustrate the kinds of initiatives and creative thinking that characterize The Boston Six effort and that should be occurring in urban-oriented colleges and universities across the country. The new projects include the following:

- The City of Boston has set up an Occupational Resource Center to provide career preparation for about 3,000 secondary and postsecondary students annually. Emphasis is to be on youth who have limited access to or who are underrepresented in Boston's technical careers programs. The Boston Six is at work

50

on a plan to join this effort in a partnership with the public schools.

- Boston's Employment and Economic Policy Administration (EEPA) has used federal entitlement funds to establish education and work-experience programs for about 4,000 in-school and out-of-school youth. The effort links EEPA with public and parochial school systems and with community organizations. Youths attend high school in public, parochial, and alternative school settings, receive assessment and counseling services, and are employed part-time. The Boston Six is developing a plan to link up with these efforts through postsecondary technical career-training programs in their community colleges in cooperation with the schools.

- Boston public schools and its Tri-Lateral Council for Quality Education (a unit of the Chamber of Commerce) have cooperated in a program for the past two years to improve career exploration and decision making among high school students. Together, they have devised curricula for teaching skills in career development and published information on job opportunities. With the Guidance Department of the Boston school system, the Tri-Lateral Council is seeking funds to expand this program to several high schools not now involved in it. The Boston Six is trying to develop a program that will use their faculty, students, and graduates to provide high school students with career information. These efforts will be integrated with those of the Tri-Lateral Council and the Guidance Department.

- As a central activity, The Boston Six is continuing the work begun during the first two grant years to develop a comprehensive system of guidance services for adults on how to enter various careers. The Boston Six is strengthening off-campus counseling and information programs, developing more active relations with private industry and state and city agencies, and designing and implementing joint approaches to the assessment of prior learning.

- The number of adults and youth in Boston who do not speak English as a native language is growing faster than any other demographic category. The Hispanic population, 20,000 in 1970, has now reached 100,000. There are numerous other ethnic groups with language problems. The schools have inadequate resources to handle in-school language needs. The Boston Six has a limited set of such services, and wants to develop expanded English-as-a-second-language programs that will link available resources across the institutions.

As this work goes forward in Boston, reorganization by the Commonwealth of Massachusetts is producing considerable confusion and disruption in the lives of The Boston Six institutions. Moreover, late in 1980 the institutions, already constrained by past state budget cuts, were hit with even further reductions. A possible consequence is that The Boston Six eventually will be consolidated into two or three. Even if this does occur, the cooperative mechanisms inaugurated by The Boston Six should continue to serve the institutions well.

CONCLUDING THOUGHTS

In stressing the need for a higher level of planning, assessment, and cooperation, one must recognize that there are constraints on how far and how fast such efforts can move. For example, in formal or informal consortia, small institutions tend to worry about losing their identity when one of the partners in the consortium is large and powerful. For real cooperation to occur, the largest institutions must be sensitive to this fear and avoid behavior that might be interpreted as condescending or preemptive by their smaller partners. At the same time, however much they may cooperate in planning and in sharing resources, institutions have their own legitimate self-interests to consider. Most can be expected to continue recruiting, counseling, and instructional programs independently of one another. The Boston Six institutions, though serious in their intent to work together in a number of areas, continue to maintain separate institutional programs in those areas. That is proper as long as each institution understands that for certain purposes their own independently operated programs and services must give way to joint action. The right balance is difficult to strike.

Finally, all of the ventures discussed in this paper occurred because external funding was available. To argue for more initiatives like them, one must acknowledge that how much the institutions can do depends in the long run on outside funding, particularly from state sources. Urban-oriented colleges and universities, like the entire educational enterprise, exist in a political environment, shaped increasingly at the state level. Yet state legislatures are often far removed from the day-to-day realities of the cities and the institutions of higher education that serve them. Much more communication is needed if legislators are to look upon the institutions with greater favor and understanding.

Costs and Funding

It may be unrealistic to think that complete educational opportunity can ever be achieved. It is indisputable, however, that the United States will have to move much farther in that direction if the problems in the cities are to be overcome. Yet we seem to be caught up in a Catch-22 situation: urban-oriented institutions compete for federal and state funds with other colleges and universities, with the public schools, and with a variety of nonacademic institutions in the city. The funds available are unable to keep pace with inflation, let alone support new initiatives. Student grant and loan programs amounting to billions of dollars a year have done little to increase the college-going rate of truly needy potential students; indeed, they are inadequate for students already enrolled in higher education. Substantially larger amounts of institutional and student aid are needed, yet the national economy continues to fluctuate and funding from traditional sources is shrinking.

It is hard to find solutions to these problems. Major improvements in the economy would be essential, but they would have to be accompanied by a strong, visible, and unswerving commitment to advancing educational opportunities for racial minorities and other disadvantaged people. Even under the difficult economic circumstances of the present, however, the performance of urban-oriented institutions could be greatly improved by changes in policy and practice. For example, a systematic review of national and state priorities and policies could reduce duplication of programs and suggest ways to develop new funding patterns. A better understanding of urban-oriented colleges and universities, and of the cities themselves, by national and state policy makers could lead to more equitable funding. By simplifying eligibility requirements for aid and loan programs and by monitoring the results more carefully and sensitively, programs could more effectively reach the people who need them most.

INSTITUTIONS: HIGHER COSTS AND UNDERFUNDING

A 1978 study by the National Center for Higher Education Management Systems (NCHEMS) calculated, on a per-student basis, federal revenues received by the nonurban and urban campuses of two universities—the Urbana and Chicago Circle campuses of the University of Illinois and the Amherst and Boston campuses of the University of Massachusetts. The study found that in both federal appropriations and federal grants and contracts the nonurban campuses received substantially more funding per student than did the urban campuses.[14] The National Association of State Universities and Land Grant Colleges, which annually examines state tax support for higher education, reported in its 1979–1980 study that the nonurban campuses cited above got substantially more state tax revenue support per student than the urban campuses.[15] The NCHEMS study reported the same finding.[16] Both studies indicate that these are not isolated examples of funding discrepancies.

Although these and other studies suggest inequities in funding, they cannot be taken as proof of unfairness. There are such wide variations in institutional budgeting and accounting practices, state and federal funding formulas, and educational operating assumptions, that figures comparing costs and revenue are almost always open to question. Although there is no question that the nonurban campuses in Illinois and Massachusetts get more federal and state support on a per-student basis, it is not at all clear what the funds are used for.

The important point is whether urban-oriented institutions of higher education are funded at a level adequate to meet the full costs of programs and services for their inner-city constituents. It should be kept in mind that because urban-oriented institutions have higher overhead costs, a smaller proportion of their total revenue is available for instructional programs and services. One of their higher costs is debt service.

During the last two decades many urban-oriented colleges and universities undertook major construction to provide more space and programs. Others were built from scratch, with total campuses constructed seemingly overnight. For example, the Boston campus of the University of Massachusetts was built entirely in 1975. (In contrast the Amherst campus evolved over the course of a century.) Whether expanding or starting fresh, urban-oriented institutions were obliged to purchase expensive land and pay high labor and construction costs. (Such costs are always higher in the cities than in rural and suburban areas.)

Thus, older, nonurban institutions that grew slowly over decades have been able to amortize their costs gradually and to pay debt service in cheaper dollars. Urban-oriented institutions, on the other hand, have had to repay building costs in a relatively short period of time and during periods of spiraling inflation. Because more of their revenue goes toward repayment of debt service than is the case with other colleges and universities, instructional programs and services are underfunded.

There are other cost differentials as well. Because the needs of their students are unconventional, with many having to work part-time, urban-oriented institutions must keep their facilities open for longer hours. Typically, classes and services are available well into the evening and on weekends. Naturally that raises utility costs, which in any case are higher in cities. To further distort the picture, utility costs are sometimes included in operating budgets and sometimes not. This makes generalizations about average costs suspect.

City economics affect operating costs in other ways not always accounted for adequately. For example, the high cost of city living results in correspondingly higher faculty and staff salaries. Unionization, a force strong in cities, is responsible for higher costs among certain categories of personnel—maintenance workers, for example.

These are costs, of course, over which urban-oriented institutions of higher education have no control. The dynamics of the city require them to provide education where the people are concentrated. Neither the institutions nor the clientele have a choice in the matter. In addition, the people that the institutions exist to serve, particularly the poor and disadvantaged, cost more to serve. As shown earlier, their students and potential students need special counseling, remedial work, and related services over and above those offered in traditional degree programs to traditional students. These things make the cost of doing business in the city greater than elsewhere. The problem is that these extra expenses are not usually factored into comparative cost analysis (partly because the data to support them are not available). Neither are they taken into account when funding decisions are made.

Another problem is insufficient information about the costs of different types and levels of educational programs. Graduate courses are often more expensive than undergraduate courses; laboratory instruction costs more than classroom lectures, and upper division instruction more than lower division instruction. Physical sciences are costlier than the humanities.

These generalizations are true in all higher education, but for reasons cited above, the costs in most categories are probably higher for institutions in the cities on a per-student basis than they are for those rural and suburban areas. The important point is that data comparing institutional costs are vulnerable because they are usually based on the assumption that programs are comparable when, in fact, the evidence for making that assumption is lacking. Nor, as a rule, are cost figures broken down by educational level or program type. Sometimes they are not provided on an institution-by-institution basis according to the same criteria. Some institutions include their medical schools and other such programs in general operating budgets; others do not. Thus, cost and funding studies are often forced to compare apples and oranges.

This situation is further complicated by full-time equivalency (FTE) formulas. This paper has indicated in general why FTE averaging does not accurately reflect the costs that institutions bear in services to part-time students and those with learning problems. More specifically, we see two kinds of problems. First, there is wide variation in FTE funding formulas among the states and the federal government. All of the states convert part-time students to full-time equivalents in some way. The U.S. Department of Education equates three part-time students to one full-time equivalent, but state ratios diverge widely from this norm.[17] Although the concept of equivalency takes into account that some students are full-time and some part-time, valid comparisons become impossible if the equivalency ratio of part-time and full-time students is not standardized.

Second, FTE figures are not very useful when related to costs. A college that has a high proportion of part-time and disadvantaged students is likely to have higher costs than a college with mostly full-time students. Put another way, the special services and programs needed by the part-time and unconventional learner are expensive to maintain and have no relation to how many credit hours the student takes. FTE averaging does not truly reflect the costs of providing educational services and programs for different clientele in different settings. This is one reason, incidentally, why comparative cost studies that provide figures on a per-student basis are not entirely convincing.

The answer to such problems is obvious. Budgeting, accounting, and funding formulas are needed that: (1) are more consistent across institutional types, interstate lines, and government levels; (2) take account of the variations in geographic location and the accidents of timing that affect debt-service levels and other uncontrollable expense elements; and (3) focus on actual costs of instruction by program type and level.

Greater consistency in all of these areas would make meaningful cost and revenue comparisons possible and help to assure that the undergraduate and compensatory programs of urban-oriented institutions of higher education are funded at a level necessary to cover the costs.

There is another good reason for improving the data base. Urban-oriented institutions will have to reassess their established educational priorities if they are to improve their response to the inner-city poor and disadvantaged. Consideration should therefore be given to whether some of the funds now channeled into graduate or other high-cost programs in these institutions might not be spent more productively on compensatory and undergraduate programs. This suggestion will be criticized by those who staunchly defend graduate education or who think that their programs are more necessary than those of others. Nevertheless, comprehensive reassessment of graduate programs in urban-oriented institutions is urgently needed.

One final point should be made. Two-year and community colleges located in the cities bear an especially large responsibility for providing compensatory education for the poor and disadvantaged. Their problems are even more severe than those faced by four-year urban-oriented colleges and universities. Nevertheless, some studies indicate that federal, state, and local funding for two-year institutions is not being maintained at the same rate as that for four-year colleges and universities in the inner city. That disparity has obvious implications for instructional programs in the two-year colleges.

STUDENTS: AID AND LOAN PROGRAMS

Student aid and loan programs designed to equalize educational opportunity actually restrict the participation of the poor in higher education. The U.S. Bureau of the Census reported in 1978, for example, that youth from low-income families are still only half as likely as middle- or upper-income youth to attend college. There are many reasons for the low participation rate, but before considering some of them, we have some general observations about the current predictions of declining enrollments in higher education during the 1980s and beyond.

Declining Enrollments in Perspective. The present debate about whether college and university enrollments can be expected to decline seems to us to divert attention from the real issue. There seems to be a general belief that if institutional resources can be maintained at present levels, the participation rate of various groups will somehow level out. But this line of thinking assumes that institutions will (or should) continue to behave much as they do now. It also tends to assume that the only people who matter are those customarily served by the system of higher education: their numbers can easily be determined and their academic behavior foreseen.

Present practices of predicting enrollments are more a reflection of what *is* than what *should be* and what *might be possible* if institutional programs, state and federal funding policies, and student financial aid programs responded better to things as they are. The attitude seems to be that signs of a decline in enrollment mean there are fewer people to educate. This interpretation reflects traditional assumptions about who should be educated and what programs they need. Never mind that there are hundreds of thousands—particularly in the cities—whose needs are unconventional, whose deprived circumstances block their path to higher education, whose lack of requisite training bars them from jobs they could otherwise perform, and whose number cannot be counted precisely anyway because there is no single standard for doing so.

When we said earlier that 75 percent of Boston's high school graduates do not go to college and that about 12 percent of the city's high school youth drop out before graduation each year, we were talking about an accumulation of thousands of individuals who are not commonly included in enrollment projections. The pattern repeats itself in cities across the country. Moreover, while the problems of unemployed urban youth cry out for attention, there are also other groups to consider. There are women who want to return to work after years of child-rearing; single mothers who must work out of economic necessity but are stuck in low-paying jobs because they are undereducated; recent immigrants who neither speak nor write English and are undercounted in all statistics; minorities locked into ghettoes because of racism; future casualties of the school system; and people of all sorts whose past learning has been rendered obsolete owing to advances in knowledge and technology.

Problems in Implementing Loan and Financial Aid Programs. In a project funded by the Ford Foundation in 1979, the Washington Office of the College Board undertook a study of the impediments to fuller use of available loan and aid programs by the urban poor. According to some national studies, there is a direct relation between the criteria and administration of the programs and the low rate at which poor and disadvantaged people take part in higher education. The study was concerned primarily with the process by which low-income urban students apply for and receive financial aid. It was based on the experience of counselors, students, and parents served by the Educational Opportunity Center (EOC) located in the predominantly black district of Anacostia in Washington, D.C.

58

A full report on the study was completed in early 1980.* It documents two broad problems that restrict use of available financial aid by the poor and disadvantaged and discourage their enrollment in college. The problems are: (1) the financial aid system itself is very complex and has unintended negative impacts on the very people it is designed to help, and (2) the services providing information and counseling about financial aid are inadequate.

Complexities of the System. The study points out that student financial aid in the United States is a combination of federal, state, and institutional systems. Each has its own eligibility criteria, application procedures and forms, standards for assessing financial need, deadlines, and administrative requirements. The result is a maze of overlaps and inconsistencies that would confuse even the most persistent and self-assured applicant. Among the specific problems pinpointed by the study are the following:

- The use of multiple forms, each asking for different information, amounts to excessive paperwork and requires more sophistication than most low-income individuals possess.

- The forms contain questions that low-income families cannot understand (because the questions use middle-class terms and income descriptions) or that call for financial information applicants cannot provide (because they do not keep adequate records).

- Deadlines for applying vary greatly from program to program, and applicants have trouble keeping track of the different requirements. Delays in filing and processing the applications keep students waiting for so long that they either drop the whole thing, lose out on aid because earlier applicants have already used up available funds, or lose their place in a college because they learn too late that they will get the aid they need.

- A new procedure of "edit checks" was introduced by the Basic Educational Opportunity Grant (BEOG) program in the academic year 1978–1979 to reduce fraud and abuse in the financial aid system. Because many questions are likely to be raised by the financial information provided by low-income people, their applications are especially vulnerable to audit. Thus they are apt

*The report was published by the Ford Foundation under the title *Student Aid and the Urban Poor* (1981).

to be disqualified even though their need for aid is both urgent and legitimate.

· Lack of continuity is another problem. Modifications of financial aid programs occur annually, sometimes in the middle of an application period. As a result, counselors and administrators cannot keep up to date.

Inadequate Informational and Counseling Services. All of the grant projects discussed in this paper cited the need for more and better counseling and information. The College Board study found tangible evidence of inadequacies in information and counseling about financial aid. The study concluded that the paucity of such services is a major obstacle to the fuller use of financial aid programs by the urban poor and by impoverished and disadvantaged students generally. The study found, for example, that:

· State and federal aid administrators do not distribute information as widely as they should. For example, only 30 percent to 40 percent of all high schools and libraries in the country receive BEOG information and applications. Even when they are provided there is no advice on how students can get help in filling out the forms.

· Counseling in colleges and high schools is small-scale and ineffective. Aid officials have limited contact with students and prospective students, are called upon to counsel more students than they can handle, and must provide psychological guidance for which they are not trained. They do not adequately explain differences in various forms of aid. Indeed, many do not fully understand the differences themselves.

· Community-based counseling services that are federally funded are not as widely available as they should be. Because of low funding, there are only 32 Educational Opportunity Centers, 153 Talent Search projects, and 413 Upward Bound programs nationwide. Moreover, existing services cannot afford proper training for the personnel.

On the basis of the findings, the College Board study recommended several measures to streamline the application process and to promote greater consistency among aid programs. It also recommended steps to improve communications with students and to personalize and expand information and counseling services across the nation— particularly community-based programs that have already demonstrated high promise.

60

The College Board study is, to be sure, a limited look at one aspect of a complex problem. Much more research like it is required as a basis for assuring proper monitoring of the system and producing refinements in it. There are, for example, problems in eligibility that present difficulties for low-income people. One is the way in which welfare and other public assistance programs are factored into students' eligibility for financial aid. A recent study by Nancy R. Mudrick explored this matter. One of her findings was that the receipt of financial aid often leads to reductions in vital public assistance benefits; public officials inappropriately count student aid as part of total family income and cut benefits accordingly, thereby penalizing families already at the edge of poverty.[18] Much more attention should be given to this problem and others like it.

It will take time to sort out and to correct the problems that poor people have with financial aid programs. Fortunately, many political and educational leaders recognize the need for corrective measures and are trying to develop them. Unfortunately, even as such efforts go forward, some financial aid experts predict that as the Education Amendments of 1980 are implemented, financial aid programs will be tilted even more toward the middle class. In an article[19] in *Change* magazine in 1980, Lawrence E. Gladieux pointed out some of the problems to watch for:

- As Congress attempts to bring the spiraling costs of aid and loan programs under control, budget trade-offs may be made, resulting in funding programs for middle- and upper-middle income students (owing to new standards for measuring need) at the expense of programs to equalize educational opportunity.

- Eligibility requirements for BEOG and campus-based federal aid will hurt low-income people because the new legislation will require larger contributions than were required in the past from families with annual incomes below $15,000.

- Although the new federal standard aims to enlarge eligibility and extend it to new groups, Congress may, in fact, not appropriate enough money each year to cover all the awards for which students qualify. The authorizing legislation contains a provision to protect the grants of neediest people in such a situation, but there is no guarantee that the provisions will be followed. Similar provisions have been ignored in the past.

- Colleges and universities can be expected to adopt a variety of responses to the new federal standard for measuring need. Many will choose to adopt the federal standard entirely and to adapt their own assistance programs to it—partly because there is a need for consistency and partly because that will enhance enrollment objectives.

Whether changes of this sort will actually occur and, if so, to what extent is hard to predict. But clearly the new federal legislation will add new problems of interpretation and application to those that already exist. Moreover, a conservative Congress bent on reducing the tax burden created by federal financial aid and inclined to relieve pressure on the middle class may not be as sensitive to the problems of poor people as it should be. It therefore behooves those who care about the problems to work with renewed vigor to help resolve them justly and equitably. Toward that end, a higher level of policy-oriented research is indicated, and much more attention should be given to monitoring the use and administration of the aid and loan programs.

CONCLUDING THOUGHTS

Some of the changes and actions suggested in this paper can be undertaken if the institutions and legislative groups to which they apply simply make up their minds to adjust practice and policy. The changes will cost something, but they will not require any major infusion of new funds. Two examples of what can be done at relatively little cost are (1) the elimination of funding inequities where they exist and (2) steps to maximize the use of available loan and aid programs by the neediest people.

Many of the recommendations, however, cannot be implemented without major and immediate *new* funding. State and federal governments will remain the primary sources of funding for higher education. Yet we are forced to conclude that large-scale new funds are not likely to become available from these sources until there are major improvements in the economy. What government officials *can* do, at the very least, is to reexamine current patterns of resource allocation, target the resources they have more equitably, and develop criteria for funding that encourage the kinds of liaisons suggested in this paper. Efforts to reduce federal and state budgets must not be allowed to affect educational programs for the needy disproportionately. Although there are disturbing signals that this may happen, such action would amount to short-term savings with dire long-term social and economic consequences.

Still, a substantial infusion of new funds is needed *now*. Even if state and federal officials can find ways to use available funds more effectively and sensitively, what hope is there if the ceiling has been reached on their level of support? Although we do not intend to suggest a diminution of responsibility by the state or federal government, we propose two short-term solutions to meet the immediate funding problem.

One is much greater involvement in education by the private sector. There are excellent examples of the private sector and urban-oriented institutions working together both in private funding of campus programs and in cooperative educational programs. Because it is in the best interest of business and industry to have an adequately trained labor force, their increased funding of programs at urban-oriented colleges and universities should be seen as a wise and proper investment.

The other short-term solution to the immediate funding problem is for foundations to increase their support of compensatory and undergraduate education programs for the inner-city poor and disadvantaged. They should also provide support for studies to inform state and national policy. Although no foundation alone has the resources to make a dramatic difference in educational opportunity for the urban poor and disadvantaged, several foundations working together—perhaps in new partnerships forged with business and industry—could produce major results.

Inching Away from the Wall: Summary of Recommendations

In the last two decades the United States has taken major strides toward equalizing educational opportunity. Yet there are still large numbers of people who are either not served or ineffectively served by institutions of higher education. The problem is particularly acute in the central cities, where the poor and disadvantaged are concentrated. For many of them, undereducation contributes to high levels of unemployment and crime, and to the disintegration of family and community.

Urban-oriented colleges and universities are losing ground in their efforts to serve underprepared and low-income students. Many factors combine to cause this situation—confusion about their mission, resulting in poor planning at every level; minimal cooperation with schools and other city institutions; adherence to traditional methods of instruction when unconventional methods are called for; inflation and inequities in funding, the complexities of student financial aid; and finally, the special problems and needs of urban-oriented colleges precisely *because* they are located in the cities.

Based on our analyses in the preceding sections of this paper, we set out below a summary of our recommendations and the specific problems to which they are addressed.

BASIC SKILLS AND RELATED PROGRAMS AND SERVICES

The single greatest need is for a range of programs that will help the poor and disadvantaged improve their basic learning and language skills and assure their access to and success in college study, and that are geared to the realities of the job market. Current programs and services are too limited even for students already in college. To address this problem, we have four broad recommendations for urban-oriented higher education institutions:

65

- *Basic skills and English-as-a-second-language programs should be strengthened and expanded to better serve both enrolled and potential students. Programs that are closely integrated with regular content courses should be emphasized.*

- *Imaginative recruitment, testing, and placement programs should be launched in urban communities across the nation.*

- *College, high school, and community-based counseling and guidance programs should be developed and expanded, with particular emphasis given to community-based efforts and to programs that integrate career, academic, financial, and psychological support.*

- *Staff and faculty development programs should be undertaken to prepare the personnel to staff these instructional, recruitment, and counseling functions.*

INSTITUTIONAL PLANNING

Inadequate planning is the prime factor restricting institutional capacity to develop basic skills programs and other services and to attract students to them. Therefore, we recommend that:

- Urban-oriented higher education institutions develop new institutional planning approaches as a first order of business.

These new planning programs should aim to do at least four things: (a) systematically identify groups in need of access to higher education; (b) assess their educational needs (taking into account that unserved students are not a homogeneous group); (c) reshape existing programs to make them more responsive to those needs; and (d) take account of local job-market realities. For the planning programs to be fully effective, they should be undertaken as part of a comprehensive reexamination of the institution's mission, involving a thorough reassessment of current educational priorities and criteria for allocating resources.

LEARNING RESEARCH

The development of learning programs for students with nontraditional needs requires the use of new theoretical knowledge about the different ways people learn. A higher level of research is needed to develop new instructional approaches and more effective means of both diagnosing learning problems and assessing learning achievement and style. Efforts to develop the theoretical base and to apply the findings are proceeding too slowly.

- To help overcome this problem, more generous funding should be provided for learning research and its application—to be carried out by groups such as the Council for the Advancement of Experiential Learning.

INSTITUTIONAL COOPERATION

Limitations on institutional resources and a reluctance to engage in genuine cooperation with other institutions also restrict institutional ability to serve the urban poor and disadvantaged. Increased cooperation of various kinds could sharpen the collective understanding of problems and lead to new resource combinations.

- Urban-oriented colleges and universities should initiate new and stronger links to a wider range of institutions in their communities.

Of special importance in this regard are cooperative planning and action projects with business and industry, other higher education institutions, and community and government agencies. Stronger ties to the schools would also help address the learning problems of today's potential dropouts before they become tomorrow's casualties.

PROVIDING INFORMATION TO POTENTIAL STUDENTS

As programs and services are strengthened through better planning and more cooperation—making maximum use of available resources and providing coherency in the overall educational enterprise— potential students will not automatically know about them or how to take advantage of them. Therefore,

- Singly and collectively, the institutions should develop information programs that reach people at home, at work, and in the community. They should also provide follow-up counseling and guidance to help the intended beneficiaries make the best use of the information.

OVERCOMING FUNDING PROBLEMS

Urban-oriented colleges and universities are further handicapped because their compensatory undergraduate programs are not adequately funded. This paper has identified four underlying reasons for the underfunding:

First, the institutions have higher overhead costs than those that either operate outside of the city or serve better-prepared students. These extra costs are not commonly recognized or factored into budgeting decisions at the state and federal levels.

Second, the institutions follow practices that deprive them of needed revenue—for example, classifying the basic skills and other compensatory courses as "non-credit," and failing to keep records and develop budgets in a form that would permit policy analysts and budget officials to make valid cost comparisons.

Third, the full-time equivalency (FTE) funding formulas in use by the states, the federal government, and the institutions are inconsistent, making the present enrollment-driven funding approach inequitable. Relatedly, neither FTE nor headcount funding arrangements take into account that the costs of compensatory programs bear no relation to the number of credit hours a student takes.

Fourth, problems of eligibility and administration prevent the urban poor from making full use of available financial aid and loan programs. This under-use affects the financial fortunes of the institutions and lowers the college participation rate of large groups they should and might otherwise be serving.

Although strong action is required in each of these areas, we have two priority recommendations aimed at promoting more equitable and adequate financing of the institutions and their needy students.

- The institutions, along with state and federal funding sources, should work toward developing greater consistency in data collection, record keeping, operating assumptions, and funding and financial aid criteria.

- Educational research organizations should undertake additional studies of the student aid system—to monitor its effects, examine problems of implementation and use, and recommend needed changes in federal and state policy and practice.

GATHERING DATA ABOUT PROGRAMS AND PEOPLE

Efforts to act on some of these recommendations will be enhanced if more can be learned about first-rate programs currently serving the urban poor. Six model programs were presented in this paper, but many others could also be taken as guides. With Ford Foundation support, the American Association of State Colleges and Universities has begun to identify a variety of such programs in urban-oriented

68

higher educational institutions around the country, but that effort is general and not likely to provide the detailed information needed for replication. In addition, no one knows the number of people nationally who need basic skills and other compensatory programs; good basic research is needed to provide this information.

- Studies should be systematically undertaken to identify promising basic skills programs, assess them, and disseminate information about them. Studies are also needed to determine the numbers and kinds of people needing such services.

THE IMMEDIATE FUNDING CHALLENGE

Although some of these recommendations can be acted on with little or no cost, others will require a major infusion of new funds. The present national economy limits what can be expected from state and federal sources in the near future, but at the very least government agencies should reexamine current patterns of revenue allocation, target their resources more carefully, and develop more creative criteria for funding. To meet the immediate funding need, however, we propose that:

- Business and industry, which need an upgraded labor force, should provide more financial support for basic skills programs.

- Philanthropic organizations should provide funding of basic skills programs and related services in the institutions called upon to provide them. Funding should also be provided for policy research and analysis.

Conclusion

This paper has emphasized the things that urban-oriented colleges and universities, and those who develop policy affecting them, fail to do or do not do well. We recognize, of course, that institutions and people of good will and determination are struggling in cities all over the country to protect and expand higher education services for the poor and disadvantaged. Nevertheless, their backs are against the wall. Faced with problems at every turn, they need help—and they need it now.

We hope that help will be forthcoming. We are persuaded that what this nation decides to do about its cities—and what happens to *all* of the people in the cities—is connected inescapably to the future of democracy in America.

Notes

1. Harold Howe II and Associate Consultants, "The City University of New York: Facilities, Finance, and Governance," A Report to the Mayor of the City of New York, December 13, 1978, p. 10.

2. James R. Jordan, private memorandum, October 26, 1977.

3. Thomas P. Robinson, "The Urban College/University in the Eighties," *Compact* 14 (Spring 1980), p. 15.

4. Ibid.

5. James R. Jordan, "Improving Basic Skills in Birmingham: A Joint Effort by Retired Teachers, Miles College, and the Public Schools," *A Tale of Three Cities: Boston, Birmingham, Hartford* (New York: Ford Foundation, 1981), p. 47.

6. Ibid., p. 48.

7. Ibid., p. 47.

8. Gail Spangenberg, et al., "Community Outreach in Hartford: A Higher Education Program for Hispanics," *A Tale of Three Cities*, pp. 54–55.

9. "Notes on a Survey of Counselor Attitudes toward Student Financial Aid," unpublished report. (Washington, D.C.: The Washington Office of the College Board, 1979).

10. Gail Spangenberg, et al., *A Tale of Three Cities*, p. 67.

11. Adriano Falcon-Trafford, et al., "Where Do We Go From Here?" (Hartford, Conn.: La Casa de Puerto Rico, Inc., 1977).

12. Mary Kinnick, *EIC Assessment Project* (Portland, Ore.: Educational Coordination Commission, 1979).

13. Frank Baratta and John Selig, *A Cooperative Self-Assessment of Programs for the Disadvantaged in the San Francisco Consortium's Universities and Colleges* (San Francisco: The San Francisco Consortium, 1980), p. 17.

14. Marilyn McCoy and Barbara Epp, *Revenues and Expenditures, 1977-1978* (Boulder, Colo.: National Center for Higher Education Management Systems, 1978), p. 10.

15. M. M. Chambers, *Appropriations: State Tax Funds for Operating Expenses of Higher Education, 1979–1980* (Washington, D.C.: Na-

tional Association of State Universities and Land Grant Colleges, 1979), pp. 7–15.

16. McCoy and Epp, *Revenues and Expenditures*, p. 12.

17. Ibid., p. 10.

18. Nancy R. Mudrick, *The Interaction of Public Assistance and Student Financial Aid* (New York: The College Board, September 1980).

19. Lawrence E. Gladieux, "What Has Congress Wrought?" *Change* 12 (October 1980), pp. 6–7.

Ford Foundation Conference Participants
(May 1980)

Frank Bonilla, Director and Professor of Political Science, Center of Puerto Rican Studies, City University of New York

Pastora San Juan Cafferty, Associate Professor, School of Social Service Administration, University of Chicago

Lisle Carter, President, University of the District of Columbia

Robert Clodius, President, National Association of State Universities and Land Grant Colleges

Fred Crossland, Program Officer, Division of Education and Public Policy, Ford Foundation

Evelyn Davila, Director, Educational Division, National Urban Coalition

Harold Delaney, Associate Director, American Association of State Colleges and Universities

Susan Fratkin, Director of Special Projects, National Association of State Universities and Land Grant Colleges

Lawrence E. Gladieux, Director, Washington Office of The College Board

Harold Howe II, Vice President, Division of Education and Public Policy, Ford Foundation

Samuel Husk, Executive Vice President, Council of Great City Schools

James Jordan, Special Advisor to the President, American Council on Education

Ernest Lynton, Senior Vice President for Academic Affairs, University of Massachusetts

William Maxwell, President, Jersey City State College

Edward Meade, Jr., Program Officer, Division of Education and Public Policy, Ford Foundation

Joseph O'Neill, Executive Secretary, Conference of Small Private Colleges

Benjamin Payton, Program Officer, Minority Higher Education, Division of Education and Public Policy, Ford Foundation

Lois Rice, Vice President, Washington Office of The College Board

Kurt Smith, Project Director, Urban College and University Network Project, American Association of State Colleges and Universities

Gail Spangenberg, Independent Education Consultant

Stephen Trachtenberg, President, University of Hartford

W. Clyde Williams, President, Miles College

Roger Yarrington, Vice President, American Association of Community and Junior Colleges

Ford Foundation Grants

RESEARCH AND DISSEMINATION

1. **American Association of State Colleges and Universities**   **$168,156 in 1978**

   To gather and disseminate information about programs offered by urban-oriented colleges and universities to serve the urban poor and disadvantaged.

2. **The College Board (Washington, D.C. Office)**   **$25,000 in 1978**
   $245,792 in 1982

   Studies of financial aid to low-income urban students. Study of the relation between the academic needs of low-income students and institutional programs intended to serve them.

3. **National Association of State Universities and Land Grant Colleges**   **$19,240 in 1981**

   To develop collaboration between city schools and urban universities.

PILOT AND DEMONSTRATION PROJECTS

1. **Alverno College**   **$22,925 in 1981**

   For a study by the Catholic colleges of Milwaukee (Alverno, Cardinal Stritch, and Mount Mary), to determine the feasibility of developing a "downtown school" to serve the increasing numbers of disadvantaged minorities in greater Milwaukee.

2. **The Boston Six**   **$148,000 in 1978**

   For inter-institutional cooperation among six public higher education institutions in Boston to improve services to the inner-city poor and disadvantaged. Projects include joint planning, counseling, and course registration.

3. **City College of New York** (City University of New York)   **$46,666 in 1982**

   Partial support to plan administrative structure and development activities to meet the needs of CCNY's disadvantaged students.

4. **DePaul University**   **$63,840 in 1981**

   To help DePaul, Loyola University, and Mundelein College develop a system of institutional planning and collaboration to increase Hispanics' access to higher education in Chicago.

5. **University of the District of Columbia** $112,490 in 1978

For a program to diagnose student learning problems in order to make the university's remedial, guidance, and counseling programs more effective and reduce student attrition.

6. **University of Hartford** $155,200 in 1978

For a cooperative project by the University of Hartford, Hartford Community College, and Hartford State Technical College to recruit inner-city Hispanic students and to give them such special assistance as English-language training.

7. **University of Houston** $68,950 in 1981

For a collaborative project with other higher education institutions in Houston and the city's public schools to assist low-income students, Hispanics in particular.

8. **Hunter College** (City University of New York) $123,582 in 1981

To rearrange faculty schedules, class hours, counseling and other support services to better serve part-time and low-income students.

9. **Jersey City State College** $165,414 in 1978

To help Jersey City State, St. Peter's College, and Hudson County Community College retrain college faculty to improve their teaching of basic skills and English as a second language.

10. **Miles College** $165,103 in 1978

For Project SUPER (Skills Upgrading Program for Educational Reinforcement), which involves Miles, the Birmingham public schools, and a group of retired teachers who tutor small groups of secondary-school students.

11. **Roosevelt University** $60,000 in 1981

To develop a program that will help ease students' transition from Chicago's two-year colleges to the university.

12. **The San Francisco Consortium** $103,300 in 1978

To assess programs for disadvantaged students developed by the consortium's eight member institutions. A particular focus is the programs' pertinence to employment in the Bay area.

78 132